Small, Sweet, and Italian

ALSO BY MARIA BRUSCINO SANCHEZ

The New Lasagna Cookbook:
A Crowd-Pleasing Collection of Recipes from
Around the World for the Perfect One-Dish Meal

Sweet Maria's Italian Cookie Tray

Sweet Maria's Cookie Jar

Sweet Maria's Cake Kitchen

Sweet Maria's Italian Desserts

Tiny, Tasty Treats from

Sweet Maria's Bakery

Small, Sweet, and Italian

Maria Bruscino Sanchez

St. Martin's Press

New York

SMALL, SWEET, AND ITALIAN. Copyright © 2013 by Maria Bruscino Sanchez. All rights reserved. Printed in the United States of America. For information, address St. Martin's Press, 175 Fifth Avenue, New York, N.Y. 10010.

www.stmartins.com

Design by Kathryn Parise

Library of Congress Cataloging-in-Publication Data

Sanchez, Maria Bruscino.
    Small, sweet, and Italian : tiny, tasty treats from Sweet Maria's Bakery / Maria Bruscino Sanchez.—First U.S. Edition.
        pages cm
    Includes bibliographical references.
    ISBN 978-1-250-02667-5 (hardcover)
    ISBN 978-1-250-02668-2 (e-book)
    1. Desserts—Italy.   2. Confectionery—Italy.   3. Baked products—Italy 4. Baking—Italy.   5. Sweet Maria's (Bakery)
I. Title.
    TX773.S26 2013
    641.860945—dc23

                                                        2013013555

St. Martin's Press books may be purchased for educational, business, or promotional use. For information on bulk purchases, please contact Macmillan Corporate and Premium Sales Department at 1-800-221-7945, extension 5442, or write specialmarkets @macmillan.com.

First Edition: September 2013

10   9   8   7   6   5   4   3   2   1

To savoring the everyday sweetness of life

Contents

Acknowledgments

Always first, a huge thanks to my mom and dad for nurturing an Italian foodie before it was fashionable.

For Edgar, for his "Italian-ness."

Thanks to Sally Maraventano, an amazing chef, for teaching me how to teach and share these traditions that we both love.

To Roseann Tully, for her personal and professional friendship, and everyone at *Intermezzo* magazine, for making me a better writer, recipe developer, and amateur food stylist.

Scott Goodwin, your photos are beautiful. You are a pleasure to work with. Kristin Rotondo, for her very attentive eye on and off the set.

Carla Glasser, for her unwavering support and industry savvy—much appreciated. Michael Flamini, friend and editor, your vision helped shape this book. Everyone at St. Martin's Press: Olga Grlic, Bethany Reis, Leah Stewart, Vicki Lame, Elsie Lyons, Kathryn Parise, and Cheryl Mamaril.

The Sweet Maria's family, thanks for doing what you do, so I can do what I do: Bryan, Charla, Dolly, Diane, Emily, Jake, Jenn, Josh, Katie, Kellie, Mike, Sondra, and Vanessa.

Generous chefs, for sharing their recipes and techniques: Francine Bove, Aunt Ann Chillemi, Nick Mancini, Sally Maraventano, Diane Michaud, Terry Sanchez, Kellie Slavinski, Susan Tropasso.

Friends for tastings, diversions, and pep talks: Andy, Jenn, Sarah, Richard, Shelley, Susan, and Tom.

Anna Luciano, thanks for the Italian lesson.

To all the Sweet Maria fans and customers, it's my pleasure to be a part of your lives and traditions.

La Dolce Vita Means "The Sweet Life"

The sweet life is different for everybody. Savoring it is what's important. For me, the sweet life is living my dream every day in my own bakery.

My life as Sweet Maria started in a close-knit Italian-American neighborhood. I was surrounded by my grandmother, her sister, her sister-in-law, her cousin, and more relatives. It was a great way to grow up, with a huge extended family that helped nurture my budding passion for baking. I learned how to bake the traditional holiday desserts at home, but it wasn't until my first job in a local bakery that I learned more about cake decorating and full-scale bakery production. I pursued a career in marketing but always kept my passion for baking alive, making cakes for family and friends in a home-based business. When I opened Sweet Maria's in 1990, it finally gave me a chance to bake things in my own style, drawing inspiration from my Italian upbringing and incorporating my favorite flavors. Plus it gave me a chance to really connect with people, families, and community in a way that only happens through food.

This book spotlights my style of combining Old World traditions with New World flavors and my world presentations. And best of all, they are tasty mini treats.

"GOOD THINGS COME IN SMALL PACKAGES" OR "SIZE MATTERS"

I've always believed this. Many people think of jewelry, but I always think of sweets. It's the little things in life that make it sweeter. When I bake and give a package of small cookies to a friend, their smile and surprise are always worth the effort.

Mini everything has taken hold of the entire baking industry. Ever since the cupcake boom, everything from doughnuts to scones to whoopie pies has gone mini. It's a trend that is definitely here to stay.

Miniature desserts are a delicious way to enjoy a treat. Small portions and Italians may not be obvious companions. I grew up in a family where small portions means a meal to serve twelve! Many of us love keeping up traditions, yet our lifestyles have changed to eat smaller and lighter. By baking minis, you can have it all: flavor, tradition, and variety.

I also grew up playing with dolls and enjoyed many hours with my miniature dollhouse. In this dollhouse everything seemed sweeter because it was tiny. It was my own little world to fuss over. I think that early fascination with small things may have shaped my current obsession with downsized desserts.

Small bites are hard to resist for a lot of reasons. They are the perfect serving size, and seem to be baked just for you, with no sharing necessary. They offer less guilt and fewer calories just by virtue of their size, are easy to prepare, and have short baking times. Small sweets can also satisfy a big craving. When I need a sugar fix, I'll reach for a mocha chip biscottini, and I keep some handy in my cookie jar for the next coffee break. With smaller sweets it's easier to sample two or three desserts. Indulge—they're tiny!

Most times I am impressed by how special the smaller versions of these sweets can be. Placed in a paper liner or not, small cakes, pastries, and pies are just cuter. Even when I have a stressful day in the bakery, I can frost a batch of mini pumpkin cupcakes and still smile. That's how I know I'm still in the right business.

LA DOLCE VITA MEANS "THE SWEET LIFE"

Introduction

Most everyday Italian desserts are fresh fruit, nuts, a simple biscotti, espresso, or a glass of sweet wine. Our famous fancy pastries are usually tied to a specific holiday or saint's feast day, meant to be shared in a big way. Desserts like cannoli, cassata, and rum baba are usually bought in pastry shops and not baked at home. With many of the recipes here, I'll guide you to have your own personal *pasticerria a casa* or "pastry shop at home."

I'm sure our grandmothers would be proud that traditions can be kept in new, interesting ways and in new proportions to fit our lifestyles and palates. Maybe not everyone in the family wants a piece of the 10-inch Easter Wheat Pie you slaved over. By baking them into tiny tarts you can keep the tradition alive and serve them at your Easter feast, a sweet way to connect the generations.

This book is not meant to be a dictionary or travelogue of all Italian sweets. With so many regional specialties, my advice is to eat your way from the top to the boot and try them all. Rather, this collection is a tasty sampling of my favorites from family and friends, and sheer inspiration from fresh simple ingredients. Small desserts, but big flavor and big traditions. Now that's a taste of the sweet life.

INGREDIENTS/PANTRY

FLOUR

ALL-PURPOSE FLOUR

All-purpose flour is used for most of the recipes in this book, unless otherwise
specified. It is readily available and most major brands work fine in these recipes.

CAKE FLOUR

Cake flour gives cakes their light texture and fine crumb. It has less gluten than
all-purpose flour. Try not to use self-rising cake flour. This is flour that already includes baking powder. I prefer to add my own amount of leavening.

DOUBLE ZERO FLOUR "00"

Doppio Zero or "00" flour is an Italian flour used mostly for pasta, pizza, and bread making. It is a very refined, soft flour, but with a high amount of protein. Many brands imported from Italy can be expensive and hard to find. A good substitute is half cake flour and half all-purpose flour. This combination will give you the same results as double zero flour. I recommend it for making Traditional Sicilian Cannoli shells.

SUGAR

GRANULATED SUGAR

Regular granulated sugar is fine for these recipes. It has great flavor and blends easily with butter and other ingredients.

CONFECTIONERS' SUGAR

Confectioners' sugar is powdered sugar. It is graded according to how finely it's ground. 10-X and 6-X are readily available and blend well with other ingredients for smooth icings and glazes. A dusting of confectioners' sugar on top of desserts is a simple way to finish them.

BROWN SUGAR

Brown sugar is granulated sugar processed with molasses for a rich flavor. It comes in light brown and dark brown, and you can use either in these recipes. Be sure to lightly pack it when measuring and break up any lumps before adding it to a recipe.

EGGS

Extra-large, grade A eggs are used for these recipes.

EGG WASH

"Egg wash" is a professional baking term for a glaze made of lightly beaten eggs with a bit of liquid added. I use 1 egg and 2 tablespoons of water. Beat lightly with a fork and brush on baked goods before baking as directed. This will give you a professional "GBD" look to your sweets—"GBD" is a Sweet Maria term for "golden brown and delicious." Egg wash can be refrigerated in an airtight container for 1 to 2 days.

BUTTER AND OILS

BUTTER

Always use unsalted butter for baking. It is fresher and offers the fullest flavor. It's easier to control the amount of salt added to each recipe. With salted butter you are never really sure how much has been added.

NONSTICK BAKING SPRAY

Always have a can of nonstick baking spray handy. You will need it to spray pans, cannoli tubes, and more for easy removal of baked goods from pans. Spray a baking sheet with nonstick baking spray, then line it with parchment paper.

VEGETABLE OIL

Some of the recipes use vegetable oil in the batters or doughs. A simple, neutral-tasting oil, such as canola or soybean oil, is fine.

CANOLA OIL FOR FRYING

Many of the recipes in this book are for fried pastries. Canola oil has a clean, neutral taste and will let the flavor of the pastry come through.

FRESH FRUIT

Many of the desserts use fresh berries or peaches, apples, and pears. Think seasonally, as most of the fruit can be interchanged depending on which fruit is available. Take advantage of the bounty in your region—that's the Italian way. Visit farms and farmers' markets to see what looks good and is ripe. Then plan your menus accordingly.

NUTS

ALMONDS, WALNUTS, HAZELNUTS

Try to keep a fresh supply of nuts on hand. If you don't use them often, try to buy a small amount, or just enough to accommodate your recipe. Many of my customers who do cookie swaps will use the "bulk buddy system." They purchase the nuts in bulk, and then share with each other.

CHESTNUTS

Chestnuts can be roasted or boiled to remove shell and skin (see box, page 65).

PUFF PASTRY

There are many brands of premade frozen puff pastry. Experiment to find the brand you like best.

LEAVENERS

BAKING POWDER AND BAKING SODA

Be sure that your supply of these chemical leaveners is fresh. Store separately in airtight containers for freshness.

YEAST

Yeast is a natural leavener used in a few of our sweet doughs. When working with yeast, it's important to know that when you are activating it, too much heat will kill the yeast and not enough heat will delay its activation. Be sure to keep a fresh supply in the refrigerator.

FLAVORINGS

SPICES

Keep a fresh supply. This is tricky if you don't bake or use them often. Try to buy spices in small quantities to ensure freshness, or use the "bulk buddy system" to share large quantities with friends.

EXTRACTS, OILS, AND LIQUEURS

These are all flavoring agents used in baking.

Pure extracts are produced by steeping the ingredient in alcohol. You can keep extracts at room temperature and they have a longer shelf life than oils.

Flavor oils are the essential oils squeezed from the ingredient itself. Most are interchangeable with extracts. Oils are more flavorful, so use a bit less when substituting. Be sure to keep oils refrigerated after opening and use them fairly quickly. They won't last as long as extracts.

Liqueurs such as amaretto, anisette, and Limoncello are staples in the Italian liquor pantry. I use these liqueurs like extracts occasionally to add a more subtle flavor to baked goods.

CITRUS PEELS

Citrus peels provide a rich flavoring and are very common in Italian desserts, especially those that originated in the south of Italy, where citrus is plentiful. When grating citrus zest, be sure to avoid the white, fleshy, bitter pith that is underneath the rind.

CANDIED CITRUS PEEL

Candied peel of lemons and oranges are like sweet natural gumdrops. Use them to garnish cassata and other traditional desserts.

COOKIE CRUMBS

If your biscotti ends and less-than-fresh amaretti are left over, they make excellent cheesecake crusts, or toppings for panna cotta, gelato, crostata, semifreddo, Italian Ricotta Cheesecakes, and more. In a food processor, simply pulse a few times for toppings. Pulse more for fine crumbs for crusts or coatings.

CHOCOLATE

Dark or semisweet chocolate is used for many of these recipes. You can certainly interchange chocolates according to your personal preference. Many high-quality brands of chocolate baking bars are readily available in most supermarkets. Many times I use semisweet chocolate chips. These are always in my pantry.

COCOA

Unsweetened Dutch-process cocoa is recommended for these recipes. It has a richer, deeper color and flavor.

CHEESE

Ricotta and mascarpone cheeses are the most popular cheeses used in Italian desserts.

Ricotta in Italian means "re-cooked." It is a slightly sweet soft cheese made from the whey of cow's milk. It is used in a variety of desserts, including cheesecakes, cassata, cannoli, and more. When I was growing up it was a perfect breakfast or snack when spread on toasted bread and sprinkled with cinnamon and sugar. Experiment with brands available in your area. Look for a whole-milk ricotta that is firm and smooth, with less moisture.

Mascarpone cheese should be soft, creamy, and smooth. It's famous for its starring role in tiramisu, but I love it in frostings and cream puffs, too.

HEAVY CREAM

Heavy cream is best for making whipped cream for desserts. It has a minimum fat content of 36 percent and doubles in volume when whipped. Try to find heavy cream that is just pasteurized as opposed to ultrapasteurized. It is fresher and will whip up stiffer than other creams. A chilled bowl and wire whisk will also help cream whip up faster and stiffer.

EQUIPMENT

Here are a few suggestions for some baking equipment to have available to make your baking easier.

UTENSILS

Because the baked goods in this book are made in smaller portions and sizes, small tools are important. Stock up on small ladles, ice-cream scoops, household teaspoons, and small spatulas. Ice-cream scoops are ideal for portioning batter into cupcake liners. Microplane graters are great for grating citrus zest finely. For larger or longer shreds, use a four-holed zester.

MIXERS

STAND MIXERS

Every kitchen should have one. For most home baking, a 4- or 5-quart mixer is a sufficient size. Using a stand mixer frees you from the mixing by allowing you to walk away from it to prep other parts of the recipe. This is especially time-efficient when you are mixing sponge cakes for 10 to 12 minutes, or incorporating air into a buttercream for 10 minutes. While these things are mixing, you can scale out other ingredients, prepare baking pans, or get ahead on cleanup.

I use a paddle attachment (or a hand mixer) unless otherwise specified in a recipe. The wire whisk attachment (or a hand mixer) is great for mixing sponge cake and whipping cream.

HAND MIXERS

Just because you have a fancy stand mixer doesn't mean that you don't need a hand mixer, too. These are essential for mixing items over water on top of a double boiler, for sweets like our semifreddo.

FOOD PROCESSORS

Many of the doughs for crust are made in the food processor. A processor is also useful for chopping nuts and dried fruits.

PARCHMENT PAPER

Almost everything I bake is on a parchment paper–lined baking sheet. You don't have to stress about greasing the pan too much or too little. Plus, parchment paper makes cleanup a whole lot easier. If you buy parchment paper on a roll, it might be too curly to lie flat on your baking sheet. Simply spray the baking sheet with non-stick baking spray, then adhere the parchment to the sheet.

BAKING SHEETS

Heavy-duty, sturdy baking sheets are always essential. When making small-portion desserts, I find it much easier to put a small cupcake pan onto a sturdy baking sheet and then place it in the oven. This makes maneuvering small pans much easier. Plus it will keep your oven cleaner in case of any spills. Use aluminum foil sheets, doubled in strength for filling and prepping desserts before plating, but not for baking.

CUPCAKE PANS

Many of the desserts in the Cupcakes Italiano chapter are baked in regular-size cupcake pans (aka muffin pans) or minis. In general, the regular-size pans have ½-cup capacity cups and the mini cupcake pans have ⅛-cup capacity cups.

TART PANS/PIE PANS

Small tart pans are available in many sizes. I use 4-inch round or rectangular tart pans with removable bottoms for a few of the recipes. I also use a ¼-cup capacity, nonstick pie pan, measuring about 2½ inches in diameter. Each recipe will guide you to the right-size pan. Small stoneware dishes can also be used for many of the pie and tart recipes. They can be baked and served in the dish.

PAPER LINERS

Paper liners are essential for baking cupcakes and mini cupcakes. You can use plain paper, foil, or greaseproof liners. These liners come in a wide assortment of colors and patterns (see sources, page 165). I prefer standard white because it show-cases the sweets simply. Use a fresh liner to plate desserts as well to give them a bakery look at home, or *pasticerria a casa*.

OVENS

Convection versus thermal. A convection oven is great because the fans allow heat to circulate throughout the oven. This means that you can have more than one shelf baking evenly at the same time. It's a real time-saver if you are doing heavy-duty baking. Otherwise a conventional oven works fine; just bake one shelf at a time.

CANNOLI TUBES

These metal tubes are used to form cannoli and cream horns. The dough is wrapped around the tube and then fried or baked. You can find them at most restaurant supply stores.

FLUTED PASTRY CUTTER

A fancy-edged pizza cutter, or pastry cutter, makes fancier dough strips for lattice-topped pies.

WIRE RACKS

Wire racks are needed to cool cakes and cookies.

DOUBLE BOILER OR STOVETOP BAIN-MARIE

Cooking or warming over simmering water is a gentle method that gives you more control than simply heating over a burner. I use a wide top, medium-size, stainless-steel bowl that fits securely on top of a medium saucepan. The saucepan should be half-filled with simmering water. I like to warm my eggs and sugar for sponge cake over simmering water before beating to increase volume. Melted chocolate and pastry cream can also be made using this method. It may be slower, but it offers greater control, especially for novice bakers, and there is less chance of it burning over water.

BASIC BAKING TIPS

Although I may not be a classically trained baker, there are many things I've learned, from family, from my talented staff, and much from more than twenty years of being in the industry. Because baking is much more a science than an art, it is important to measure ingredients accurately and pay attention to your recipe. Read through the recipe several times before you start. When a recipe has many components, think in terms of what you can make ahead and when you should assemble. I try to think in a backward timeline from when I am serving the dessert.

GET YOUR *MISE* TOGETHER

The classic French culinary term of *mise en place,* meaning "everything in its place," is vital for successful baking. It makes you work in a more organized manner by assembling your ingredients and placing them in sequence according to the directions before you start.

ROOM TEMPERATURE

Room-temperature ingredients are essential for most baking. Room-temperature butter will make creaming with other ingredients much easier. For sponge cake I even go one step further to warm the eggs over simmering water before beating. This will give you increased volume while mixing.

THE CREAMING METHOD

This method of mixing, or "creaming," the butter and sugar together is one of the most important techniques in baking.

1. Be sure the butter is softened enough to cream with the sugar. Press your fingertip into the butter. If the butter holds the indent, then it's soft enough.
2. Cream the butter and sugar together until light in color and texture, starting with low speed, then increasing to medium-high. It should be very pale.
3. Add the eggs and flavoring and mix until well blended.
4. Add the dry ingredients on low speed just until incorporated. Be sure to scrape down the sides and bottom of the bowl. Don't overmix the dry ingredients. This will develop the gluten in the flour and make your dough tough.
5. For some cake recipes, the dry ingredients are added alternately with some type of liquid (milk or buttermilk). After adding eggs, add the dry ingredients alternately with the liquid, on low speed, beginning and ending with the dry ingredients.

THE SPONGE METHOD

This classic method for sponge or Torta Genovese is actually quite simple.

1. Combine the eggs, sugar, and salt in a stainless-steel bowl over simmering water. Lightly whisk until the temperature reaches 110°F. This will help add volume to your sponge.
2. Transfer the egg mixture to the bowl of a stand mixer. Using the wire whisk attachment (or using a hand mixer), whip until very light, pale, and thick, 10 to 12 minutes. I always set a timer for this stage because it is so important.
3. Carefully fold in the flour, a quarter at a time, being careful not to deflate the foam.
4. Pour the mixture into the pan and bake immediately so that you don't lose any volume.
5. For cupcakes, fill the liners two-thirds full with the batter. They need room to expand as they bake.

FOLDING

My mom taught me a long time ago about the importance of folding gently. She has a sponge cake that she is famous for, and only let me fold the egg whites into this batter for her very recently. It is so important to be patient, and fold in small batches. Use a flexible spatula to gently fold and scrape the batter from underneath to the top.

TURNING DOUGH OUT

Sometimes a pie or bread dough will need some kneading. After initial mixing in a food processor or mixer, turn the dough out onto a lightly floured surface and knead in additional flour if necessary. This hands-on approach lets you feel if the dough is soft, sticky, or elastic, and it gives you more control over the dough texture.

CHOPPING NUTS

"Coarsely chopped" is a few simple pulses in the food processor to keep the nuts somewhat meaty. "Finely ground" means processing longer until fine.

FILLING A PASTRY BAG

By using a pastry bag to fill and pipe cakes and pastries you can make a great professional presentation. Pastry bags can be used fitted with a coupler and tip or can be used by cutting the tip of the bag open. Be sure to open the top of the bag wide with one hand while spooning the desired frosting or filling into the bag. Be careful not to overfill. You can always refill when needed. Gather up the folded-over edges. To use, cut off the tip of the bag to the desired size. Simply squeeze and add pressure to the center of the bag, releasing the contents from the bottom. Practice and repetition will help you regulate the size of whatever you are piping.

When piping cookies onto parchment paper, gently squeeze and press the tip of the pastry onto the paper to release the dough.

FRIED DESSERTS

Use canola oil for frying desserts. Try to regulate the temperature of the oil. A steady temperature of 350°F will give you the best results. Fried desserts such as cannoli or zeppole are best when eaten freshly fried; otherwise they get soggy.

TESTING CAKES FOR DONENESS

Most recipes will instruct home bakers that a cake is done when a cake tester comes out clean. For me, that is almost too late. I like to remove a cake or cupcake from the oven when a fine crumb sticks to the tester. The cake will continue to bake after you remove it from the oven. Always set the timer for less time than specified, and check. Windows and lights in ovens help to monitor doneness. Be careful not to overbake small cakes.

HOW TO WHIP CREAM

Heavy cream will whip up faster and firmer with a chilled bowl and a chilled whip. Start slow, and whip on medium-high until the cream is the texture of shaving cream. Gradually add sugar while mixing and beat on high until stiff. Use immediately. Try to find pasteurized cream instead of ultrapasteurized when possible. It is fresher and will whip up thicker and stiffer.

FROSTINGS

Butter-based frostings require a lot of whipping to incorporate air. This air will provide a "whippiness" that not only makes the frosting taste lighter and less grainy but will make the frosting easy to use for icing or piping onto small cakes. I use the bowl of a stand mixer fitted with the paddle attachment (or a hand mixer) on medium-high speed or the highest speed it can go without spilling the mixture out of the bowl. Set the timer for 8 to 10 minutes to be sure you are whipping it enough.

HOW TO MELT CHOCOLATE

For drizzling or dipping, microwave chocolate on high for 15 seconds, stir, and repeat in 10-second increments until melted. Or melt in a bowl over a saucepan of simmering water.

CUPCAKES 101: TIPS FOR CUPCAKE PERFECTION

- Use a ladle or ice-cream scoop to fill pans cleanly. Wipe any spills from the pans, so that paper liners don't stick to the pan during baking.
- Be careful not to overbake. Cupcakes are small and require less baking time.
- The easiest way to fill cupcakes is by using a pastry bag. Simply insert the pastry bag into the middle of the cupcake and squeeze to release the filling into the cake.
- To frost cupcakes, use a small spatula to spread frosting on top of the cupcake, or fill a pastry bag with frosting and pipe frosting onto the top of the cupcake. Start piping from the outer edge and circle in to the center.

SWEET SAMPLING EVENTS

The greatest part of baking small-size desserts is that you can bake a variety of them for a sweet sampling. Why have one huge cake in a single flavor for an occasion when you can have a little bit of a lot of sweets? It's a great idea and a big trend in wedding and special occasion dessert planning.

TIPS FOR DESSERT TABLES

When you are planning a dessert table for a party there are certain things to think about.

- *How many guests will you be serving?*
  A good rule of thumb is to have 3 to 4 servings for each person.
- *Are the sweets for take-home, too?*
  In the style of Italian showers, many people want to serve desserts plus offer take-home sweets. If this is the case, you'll need to provide a larger quantity of sweets, plus pretty bags or boxes for take-away containers. Or you can pre-package a single item for a take-home favor. This gives you more control over what is being taken and can help you with figuring out the quantities needed.
- *What are the favorite flavors of the guest of honor?*
  I always try to tailor a menu according to people's favorites. If I don't know the preferences of the guests, I'll try to include a variety of sweets, including cakes, cookies, and pastries. A good selection of flavors is important, too: something chocolate, something with fruit, perhaps, something almond or nutty, and something tart, like lemon.
- *Is there a theme?*
  An all-chocolate table, an all–traditional dessert theme, a holiday theme, or

maybe a color scheme. All-white dessert tables are popular for weddings as well as assortments of small sweets, a small tiered wedding cake, and a sampling of candies, too.

PAIRING DESSERTS WITH DESSERT WINES

- A miniature dessert buffet is a great way to experiment with pairings of dessert wines.
- My personal philosophy has always been to drink what you like. But as a general rule it's important not to overwhelm your desserts with any certain wine. The wine should enhance the experience.
- As a general rule, the darker and richer the dessert, the darker and richer the dessert wine. I occasionally like to break this rule by serving a light sparkling wine to offset a very rich dessert.
- Don't limit yourself to only Italian wines. Vin Santo, Moscato, prosecco, and Marsala are classics, but Port, Madeira, sherry, and ice wines are also fine companions to many of these desserts.
- Think light and citrus tones with amaretti, dark and rich with Torta Caprese.
- Experiment on your own, but use your local wine merchant as a resource. You might be surprised at their knowledge and enthusiasm.

Cupcakes Italiano

Cupcakes get Italianized! Many of our most popular cupcake flavors are classic Italian treats like tiramisu or cassata. Why not bake them in a perfect single serving, cupcake-style? Think outside the paper liner and try our tasty triple-layered Neopolitan, or our rich and sinful Godfather Cupcake—va bene?

Cappuccino-Hazelnut Cupcakes

Orange Polenta Cakes

Basil-Lemon–Olive Oil Cakes

Tiramisu Cupcakes

Apple Cakes *(Tortine di Mele)*

Tiny Torta Caprese

Mini Spice Cakes with Vanilla
   Mascarpone Buttercream

Almond Cakes *(Frangipani)*

Italian Ricotta Cheesecakes

Bellini Cupcakes

Godfather Cupcakes

Limoncello Cakes

Fig and Rum Holiday Fruitcakes

Mini Pumpkin Cakes *(Tortine di Zucca)*

Angel Food Cupcakes
   (Tortine d'Angeli)

Cassata Cupcakes

Neopolitan Cupcakes

Mini Christmas Panettone

Pistachio-Chocolate Cupcakes

Toasted Almond Cupcakes

Cappuccino-Hazelnut Cupcakes

My two favorite Italian flavors combine in this cupcake. This is one of our biggest sellers, especially for the holidays.

Hazelnut Cake

3 extra-large eggs

2 cups granulated sugar

1 cup vegetable oil

3 teaspoons Frangelico or other
    hazelnut liqueur

2 cups cake flour

1 teaspoon baking powder

$1/4$ teaspoon salt

1 cup buttermilk

$1/2$ cup hazelnuts, finely chopped,
    plus more for garnish

Coffee Mousse Filling

2 tablespoons boiling water

2 tablespoons instant coffee

$3/4$ cup heavy cream

$1/2$ cup granulated sugar

Chocolate-Espresso Buttercream Frosting

$1/2$ pound (2 sticks) unsalted butter,
    softened

1 cup unsweetened Dutch-process
    cocoa powder

6 cups confectioners' sugar

About 4 tablespoons strong
    brewed coffee

MAKE THE HAZELNUT CUPCAKES

1. Preheat the oven to 350°F. Line standard-size cupcake pans with paper liners.

2. In the bowl of a stand mixer fitted with the paddle attachment (or using a hand mixer), on medium-high speed, whip the eggs until fluffy. Gradually add the granulated sugar and mix until very light, 5 to 6 minutes. Gradually add the oil and Frangelico and mix until well blended.

3. In a small bowl, combine the flour, baking powder, and salt. Add the flour mixture to the egg mixture alternately with the buttermilk, beginning and ending with the flour mixture. Mix until blended.

4. Stir in the chopped hazelnuts.

5. Fill the lined cupcake pans three-quarters full with the batter.

6. Bake the cupcakes for 15 to 20 minutes, or until a cake tester inserted into the center comes out with a fine crumb.

7. Remove the pans from the oven. Carefully remove the cupcakes from the pans and transfer to wire racks to cool. Cool completely before filling and frosting.

MAKE THE FILLING

8. In a small bowl, add the boiling water to the instant coffee. Set aside.

9. In the bowl of a stand mixer fitted with the wire whisk attachment, whip the cream on medium speed until soft peaks form. Add the granulated sugar and coffee mixture and whip on high speed until stiff peaks form. Use immediately.

MAKE THE FROSTING

10. In the bowl of a stand mixer fitted with the paddle attachment (or using a hand mixer), combine the butter, cocoa, 3 cups of the confectioners' sugar, and 2 tablespoons of the coffee and beat on low speed until blended. Gradually add the remaining 3 cups confectioners' sugar and beat on high speed until fluffy, 2 to 3 minutes. If the frosting seems too stiff to use, add some additional coffee. Use immediately or store in the refrigerator in an airtight container. Let the frosting come to room temperature and re-whip before using.

ASSEMBLE THE CUPCAKES

11. Fill a pastry bag with the mousse filling. Cut the tip of the pastry bag to make a small opening. Insert the tip of the bag into the center of the cupcake. Squeeze the bag to release the mousse into the center of the cupcake. Repeat until all the cupcakes are filled.

12. Fill another pastry bag with the frosting. Pipe the frosting onto the top of each cupcake, starting at the outer edge and circling in to the center. (Or spread the frosting on top of the cupcake with a small spatula.) Sprinkle with chopped hazelnuts. Refrigerate until serving. Let the cupcakes come to room temperature for serving.

Makes 15 standard-size cupcakes

Orange Polenta Cakes

My friend Chef Francine shared this recipe with me years ago and it's become one of my "go-to" recipes. The rustic texture of yellow cornmeal is perfect with a tiny garnish of orange marmalade when you want a simple casual snack cake in the style of casalinga, *or housewife.*

Polenta Cake

3/4 cup cake flour

3/4 cup cornmeal

1 teaspoon baking powder

1/4 teaspoon salt

1/2 pound (2 sticks) unsalted butter, softened

1 1/4 cups granulated sugar

4 extra-large eggs

4 extra-large egg yolks

2 tablespoons finely chopped orange zest

Topping

Confectioners' sugar, for dusting

1 cup orange marmalade

1. Preheat the oven to 350°F. Line standard-size cupcake pans with paper liners.
2. In a small bowl, combine the flour, cornmeal, baking powder, and salt. Set aside.
3. In the bowl of a stand mixer fitted with the paddle attachment (or using a hand mixer), cream the butter and granulated sugar on medium-high speed until light. Add the eggs, one at a time, beating well after each addition. Add the egg yolks and orange zest and mix well.
4. With the mixer on low speed, add the flour mixture and mix just until blended.
5. Fill the lined cupcake pans three-quarters full with the batter.

6. Bake the cupcakes for 15 to 20 minutes, or until a cake tester inserted into the center comes out with a fine crumb. Remove the pans from the oven. Carefully remove the cupcakes from the pans and transfer to wire racks to cool. Cool completely before topping.

7. Dust the tops of the cupcakes with confectioners' sugar. Spoon a drop of orange marmalade onto the top of each cupcake. Serve at room temperature.

Makes 24 standard-size cupcakes

Basil-Lemon–Olive Oil Cakes

These slightly sweet olive oil–based cakes have a distinctive flavor and light texture. They are almost savory, ideal as the partner for a hearty soup, or as part of an antipasto buffet.

Cake

2 1/2 cups cake flour

1/2 teaspoon baking soda

1/2 teaspoon baking powder

1/2 teaspoon salt

3 extra-large eggs

1 1/2 cups sugar

1 cup extra-virgin olive oil

Finely grated zest of 2 lemons

1 cup whole milk

1 tablespoon chopped fresh basil

Topping

Juice of 2 lemons

1. Preheat the oven to 350°F. Line standard-size cupcake pans with paper liners.
2. In a small bowl, combine the flour, baking soda, baking powder, and salt. Set aside.
3. In the bowl of a stand mixer fitted with the wire whisk attachment (or using a hand mixer), beat the eggs and sugar on high speed until light and lemon colored, 5 to 8 minutes. With the mixer on high speed, stream in the olive oil until blended. Add the lemon zest.
4. Mix the flour mixture into the egg mixture alternately with the milk, beginning and ending with the flour. Stir in the basil.
5. Fill the lined cupcake pans almost to the top with the batter.

6. Bake the cupcakes for 15 to 20 minutes, or until a cake tester inserted into the center comes out with a fine crumb.

7. Remove the pans from the oven. Pour the lemon juice over the hot cupcakes. Let the cupcakes cool in the pans.

8. Remove the cupcakes from the pans and serve at room temperature.

Makes 12 to 14 standard-size cupcakes

Tiramisu Cupcakes

Everyone's favorite Italian dessert, but in cupcake form. This sponge cupcake is soaked in espresso, filled with sweetened mascarpone cheese, topped with whipped cream, and garnished with a generous sprinkling of cocoa. It's the perfect "pick-me-up" for any occasion.

Sponge Cupcakes

4 extra-large eggs, at room temperature

1 cup sugar

Pinch of salt

1$\frac{1}{4}$ cups cake flour

Topping

1$\frac{1}{2}$ cups heavy cream

$\frac{1}{2}$ cup sugar

Unsweetened Dutch-process cocoa
  powder, for dusting

Mascarpone Filling

1 pound mascarpone cheese

$\frac{1}{2}$ cup sugar

$\frac{1}{2}$ cup brewed espresso

MAKE THE SPONGE CUPCAKES

1. Preheat the oven to 350°F. Line standard-size cupcake pans with paper liners.
2. Combine the eggs, sugar, and salt in a stainless-steel bowl set over a saucepan of simmering water. Lightly whisk until the temperature of the mixture reaches 110°F. This will help add volume to your sponge.
3. Transfer the egg mixture to the bowl of a stand mixer fitted with the wire whisk

attachment and whip on high speed until very light, pale, and thick, 10 to 12 minutes. I always set a timer for this stage because it is so important.

4. Carefully fold in the flour, a quarter at a time, being careful not to deflate the foam.

5. Fill the cupcake liners two-thirds full with the batter.

6. Bake the cupcakes for 15 to 20 minutes, or until golden brown and center springs back when touched.

7. Remove the pans from the oven. Cool the cupcakes in the pans on wire racks. Cool completely before filling.

MAKE THE FILLING

8. In the bowl of a stand mixer fitted with the paddle attachment (or using a hand mixer), cream the mascarpone and sugar on medium speed until smooth. Refrigerate the filling until ready to use. (The filling can be made 1 day in advance.)

MAKE THE TOPPING

9. In the bowl of a stand mixer fitted with the wire whisk attachment (or using a hand mixer), whip the cream on high speed until soft peaks form. Gradually add the sugar and continue to beat until stiff. Use immediately.

ASSEMBLE THE CUPCAKES

10. Place the espresso in a small bowl. Working one at a time, dip the top of each cupcake into the espresso. Hold the cupcake in the espresso until the coffee soaks through the sponge, about 15 seconds. Repeat with all the cupcakes. Drizzle any remaining espresso over the cupcakes.

11. Fill a pastry bag with the mascarpone filling. Cut off the tip of the pastry bag to make a small opening. Insert the tip of the bag into the center of the cupcake. Squeeze to release the filling. Repeat until all the cupcakes are filled.

12. Fill another pastry bag with the whipped cream frosting. Cut off the tip of the pastry bag to make a small opening. Pipe the whipped cream frosting onto the tops of the cupcakes, starting at the outer edges and circling in to the centers. Dust the tops with cocoa.

13. Refrigerate until serving.

Makes 12 to 15 standard-size cupcakes

Apple Cakes

TORTINE DI MELE

When I was growing up, these cakes were a much-loved breakfast treat. The recipe is extremely flexible, so you can substitute any firm seasonal fruit in place of the apples. Be sure to use farm-fresh fruit at the peak of ripeness.

$1^{1}/_{2}$ cups all-purpose flour

$1^{1}/_{2}$ cups sugar

$^{1}/_{4}$ teaspoon baking soda

1 teaspoon baking powder

$^{1}/_{4}$ teaspoon salt

6 tablespoons ($^{3}/_{4}$ stick) unsalted butter

1 extra-large egg

4 apples, peeled, cored, and sliced

Cinnamon-sugar (2 teaspoons ground cinnamon mixed with $^{1}/_{4}$ cup sugar)

1. Preheat the oven to 350°F. Line a standard-size cupcake pan with paper liners.
2. In a food processor, combine the flour, sugar, baking soda, baking powder, and salt. Pulse until blended. Add the butter and pulse until uniform. Add the egg and pulse until slightly crumbly. It's OK if the dough doesn't really stick together.
3. Press the dough into the lined cups, filling them about three-quarters full with the dough. Top with the sliced apples. Sprinkle with the cinnamon-sugar.
4. Bake the cupcakes for 15 to 20 minutes, or until a cake tester inserted into the center comes out with a fine crumb.
5. Remove the pan from the oven. Cool the cupcakes in the pan on a wire rack. Serve at room temperature.

Makes 12 standard-size cupcakes

Tiny Torta Caprese*

A tiny taste of my favorite place! The isle of Capri, just off the coast of Naples, is the birthplace of these brownielike, flourless chocolate cakes. Don't overbake these little cakes; they need to keep their chocolate chewiness. They are a perfect dose of chocolate for any dessert buffet.

8 tablespoons (1 stick) unsalted butter

Six 1-ounce squares semisweet chocolate

4 extra-large eggs, separated

$1/8$ teaspoon cream of tartar

1 cup granulated sugar

1 cup walnuts, finely chopped

Confectioners' sugar, for dusting

1. Preheat the oven to 350°F. Line mini cupcake pans with paper liners.
2. In a double boiler or in a stainless-steel bowl set over a saucepan of simmering water, melt the butter and chocolate. Set aside to cool.
3. In the bowl of a stand mixer fitted with the wire whisk attachment (or using a hand mixer), whip the egg whites and cream of tartar on high speed until stiff peaks form, 4 to 5 minutes.
4. In another mixer bowl, whip the egg yolks and granulated sugar with the wire whisk attachment (or using a hand mixer) on high speed until light and lemon colored, about 5 minutes.
5. Add the cooled chocolate mixture to the egg yolk mixture and mix just until blended.
6. Gently fold the egg whites and nuts into the chocolate mixture.
7. Fill the lined cupcake pans with the cake batter, filling each liner to the top.

8. Bake the cupcakes for 10 to 12 minutes, or until the tops are puffed and cracked.

9. Remove the pans from the oven. Cool the cupcakes in the pans on wire racks.

10. Carefully remove the cupcakes from the pans and remove them from the paper liners. Place each one upside down in a new liner. Dust the tops with confectioners' sugar.

Makes 24 mini cupcakes

*Wheat-free

Mini Spice Cakes with Vanilla Mascarpone Buttercream

Spicy cakes have long been a favorite, especially in this tiny two-bite version topped with a tasty vanilla mascarpone buttercream. Be sure to look for a brand of mascarpone that is firm and creamy, not watery.

Spice Cupcakes

2 cups cake flour

1$^1/_2$ teaspoons baking powder

$^1/_2$ teaspoon salt

1 teaspoon ground cinnamon

$^1/_2$ teaspoon freshly grated nutmeg

8 tablespoons (1 stick) unsalted butter, softened

$^3/_4$ cups granulated sugar

2 extra-large eggs

1 teaspoon pure vanilla extract

1 cup whole milk

Vanilla Mascarpone Buttercream

4 tablespoons ($^1/_2$ stick) unsalted butter, softened

$^1/_2$ cup mascarpone cheese

3 cups confectioners' sugar

1 teaspoon pure vanilla extract

Cinnamon-sugar (1 teaspoon cinnamon mixed with 2 tablespoons sugar), for sprinkling

MAKE THE CUPCAKES

1. Preheat the oven to 350°F. Line mini cupcake pans with paper liners.
2. In a small bowl, combine the flour, baking powder, salt, cinnamon, and nutmeg. Set aside.

3. In the bowl of a stand mixer fitted with the paddle attachment (or using a hand mixer), cream the butter and granulated sugar on high speed until light. Add the eggs, one at a time, beating well after each addition. Add the vanilla.

4. Add the flour mixture to the egg mixture, on low speed, alternately with the milk, beginning and ending with the flour.

5. Fill the lined cupcake pans three-quarters full with the batter.

6. Bake the cupcakes for 12 to 15 minutes, or until a cake tester inserted into the center comes out with a fine crumb.

7. Remove the cakes from the oven. Carefully remove the cupcakes from the pans and transfer to wire racks to cool. Cool completely before frosting.

MAKE THE BUTTERCREAM

8. In the bowl of a stand mixer fitted with the paddle attachment (or using a hand mixer), cream the butter and mascarpone on low speed until smooth. Gradually add the confectioners' sugar and vanilla and beat on high speed for 5 to 8 minutes, or until very light and fluffy.

9. Use immediately or store refrigerated in an airtight container. (Bring the buttercream to room temperature and re-whip before using.)

ASSEMBLE THE CUPCAKES

10. Fill a pastry bag with the Vanilla Mascarpone Buttercream. Cut off the tip of the pastry bag to make a small opening. Pipe the buttercream onto the top of each cupcake, starting at the outer edge and circling in to the center. (Or spread frosting on top of the cupcake with a small spatula.) Sprinkle with the cinnamon-sugar.

Makes 24 mini cupcakes

Almond Cakes

FRANGIPANI

These tiny cakes are packed with a powerful dose of almond. Frangipane is a French creation, inspired by an Italian living in France who invented a fragrant almond perfume. It's easy to become addicted to these moist little cakes, but the recipe can be doubled to satisfy a big craving.

$1/2$ pound almond paste (or apricot kernel paste), broken into small pieces

$1/4$ cup granulated sugar

$1/4$ cup cake flour

8 tablespoons (1 stick) unsalted butter, softened

3 extra-large eggs

Confectioners' sugar, for dusting (optional)

1. Preheat the oven to 350°F. Line mini cupcake pans with paper liners.
2. In the bowl of a stand mixer fitted with the paddle attachment (or using a hand mixer), combine the almond paste, granulated sugar, and flour and mix on low speed until blended. Add the butter and mix until smooth. Add the eggs, one at a time, beating well on medium speed after each addition.
3. Fill the lined cupcake pans almost to the top with the batter.
4. Bake the cupcakes for 12 to 15 minutes, or until a cake tester inserted into the center comes out with a fine crumb.

5. Remove the pans from the oven. Carefully remove the cupcakes from the pans and cool on wire racks. Lightly dust the tops with confectioners' sugar, if desired.

Makes about 30 mini cupcakes

Italian Ricotta Cheesecakes

Ricotta makes Italian cheesecake lighter in texture than its American cousin. A biscotti crumb crust is a great way to use up the biscotti "ends." Simply pulse ends in a food processor until finely ground. Like most cheesecakes, these are best served the day after baking. Plus, they are easier to remove from pans on the next day. Serve in their paper liners or remove just before serving.

Garnish the cheesecakes according to the season: fresh berries in summer, or a fig and Marsala sauce in winter.

Crust

1 1/2 cups crushed biscotti crumbs
    (see page xxi)
1/4 cup sugar
6 tablespoons (3/4 stick) unsalted
    butter, melted and cooled

Cheesecake Filling

4 cups ricotta cheese
1/2 cup sugar
2 extra-large eggs
2 extra-large egg yolks

1/4 cup all-purpose flour
2 teaspoons amaretto

Topping

Fresh summer berries
    or fig and Marsala sauce (see below)

Fig and Marsala Sauce

1 cup Marsala wine
1/2 cup sugar
1 cup dried figs, coarsely chopped

MAKE THE CRUST

1. Preheat the oven to 300°F. Line a standard cupcake pan with paper liners.
2. In a small bowl, combine the biscotti crumbs, sugar, and butter and mix until uniform. Press the mixture into the lined cups.
3. Bake the crusts for 5 to 8 minutes. Remove the crusts from the oven. Cool the crusts in the pan on a wire rack.

MAKE THE CHEESECAKE FILLING

4. In the bowl of a stand mixer fitted with the paddle attachment (or using a hand mixer), combine the ricotta, sugar, eggs, egg yolks, flour, and amaretto and mix on medium speed until smooth.
5. Fill the cooled crusts to the top with the filling.
6. Bake the cheesecakes for 25 to 30 minutes, or until the tops are slightly cracked and just about set (not shaking).
7. Remove the pan from the oven. Cool the cheesecakes in the pan on a wire rack.
8. Wrap the pan in plastic wrap and refrigerate overnight.

MAKE THE FIG AND MARSALA SAUCE, IF USING

9. In a small saucepan, combine the Marsala, sugar, and figs. Bring to a boil, then reduce the heat and simmer, without stirring, until the liquid has reduced to a syrup, 15 to 20 minutes. Cool slightly. (The sauce can be made 1 to 2 days in advance. Refrigerate in an airtight container. Slowly reheat before serving.)

ASSEMBLE THE CHEESECAKES

10. Carefully remove the cheesecakes from the pan. Remove from the paper liners. Serve on individual dessert plates topped with fruit or the fig and Marsala sauce.

Makes 12 standard-size cupcakes

Bellini Cupcakes

The fresh flavors of peach and prosecco shine in this tasty cupcake inspired by the classic cocktail from Harry's Bar in Venice. They are perfect treats to brighten up a springtime brunch.

Sponge Cupcakes

4 extra-large eggs

1 cup granulated sugar

Pinch of salt

1¼ cups cake flour

Peach Cream Filling

2 cups puréed ripe peaches

¼ cup cornstarch

¼ cup heavy cream

2 tablespoons granulated sugar

1 cup prosecco or other sparkling white wine

Confectioners' sugar, for dusting

Fresh peach slices, for garnish

MAKE THE SPONGE CUPCAKES

1. Preheat the oven to 350°F. Line a standard cupcake pan with paper liners.
2. Combine the eggs, granulated sugar, and salt in a stainless-steel bowl over a saucepan of simmering water. Lightly whisk until the temperature of the mixture reaches 110°F. This will help add volume to your sponge.
3. Transfer the egg mixture to the bowl of a stand mixer fitted with the wire whisk attachment (or use a hand mixer) and whip on high speed until very light, pale, and thick, 10 to 12 minutes. I always set a timer for this stage because it is so important.

4. Carefully fold in the flour, a quarter at a time, being careful not to deflate the foam.

5. Fill the lined cupcake pan two-thirds full with the batter.

6. Bake the cupcakes for 15 to 20 minutes, or until golden brown and center springs back when touched.

7. Remove the pan from the oven. Cool the cupcakes in the pan on a wire rack. Cool completely before filling.

MAKE THE FILLING

8. In a small saucepan over medium heat, bring the peach purée and cornstarch to a boil, stirring constantly. Remove from the heat. Set aside to cool.

9. In the bowl of a stand mixer fitted with the wire whisk attachment (or using a hand mixer), whip the cream on high speed until stiff peaks form. Add the sugar. Fold the whipped cream into the peach mixture.

ASSEMBLE THE CUPCAKES

10. Pour the prosecco into a small bowl. Dip the top of a cake into the prosecco and hold for 15 seconds. Repeat with the remaining cupcakes.

11. Fill a pastry bag with the peach cream filling. Cut off the tip of the pastry bag to make a small opening. Insert the pastry bag into a cake and squeeze to release filling. Repeat until all the cupcakes are filled. Dust the tops of the cupcakes with confectioners' sugar and garnish with the peach slices.

Makes 12 standard-size cupcakes

Godfather Cupcakes

Originally designed for a Father's Day segment featuring "manly" cupcakes and inspired by the cinema classic The Godfather, *this cupcake "Italiano" features a chocolate cake to die for, filled with espresso cream and topped with ganache and a touch of sambuca whipped cream—a flavor combination you can't refuse.*

Chocolate Cupcakes

1 1/2 cups all-purpose flour

1 1/2 cups unsweetened Dutch-process cocoa powder

3 teaspoons baking powder

1/4 teaspoon salt

1/2 pound (2 sticks) unsalted butter, softened

1 1/2 cups sugar

4 extra-large eggs

1 cup buttermilk

Espresso Cream Filling

2 tablespoons boiling water

3 tablespoons instant coffee

3/4 cup heavy cream

1/2 cup sugar

Ganache

1/2 cup heavy cream

2 cups chocolate chips, finely chopped

1 tablespoon unsalted butter

Sambuca Cream

1/2 cup heavy cream

1/4 cup sugar

1/4 cup sambuca or anisette

18 chocolate-covered espresso beans, for garnish

MAKE THE CUPCAKES

1. Preheat the oven to 350°F. Line standard cupcake pans with paper liners.
2. In a small bowl, combine the flour, cocoa, baking powder, and salt.
3. In the bowl of a stand mixer fitted with the paddle attachment (or using a hand mixer), cream the butter and sugar on medium-high speed until light. Add the eggs and mix until well blended.
4. With the mixer on low speed, add the flour mixture to the egg mixture alternately with the buttermilk, starting and ending with the flour.
5. Fill the lined cupcake pans two-thirds full with the batter.
6. Bake the cupcakes for 15 to 20 minutes, or until a cake tester inserted into the center comes out with a fine crumb.
7. Remove the pans from the oven. Carefully remove the cupcakes from the pans and transfer to wire racks to cool. Cool completely before filling and frosting.

MAKE THE FILLING

8. In a small bowl, add the boiling water to the instant coffee. Set aside.
9. In the bowl of a stand mixer fitted with the wire whisk attachment (or using a hand mixer), whip the cream on medium speed until soft peaks form. Add the sugar and coffee mixture and continue to whip on high speed until stiff peaks form. Use immediately.

MAKE THE GANACHE

10. In a small saucepan, heat the heavy cream until it is simmering, but not boiling, stirring constantly. Place the chocolate chips in a small bowl. Pour the hot cream over the chocolate chips and stir to blend. Stir in the butter and continue to stir until the mixture resembles thick pudding. Use immediately or store, refrigerated, in an airtight container. To reheat the ganache, heat it in a

double boiler or in a stainless-steel bowl set over a saucepan of simmering water, stirring until smooth.

MAKE THE SAMBUCA CREAM

11. In the bowl of a stand mixer fitted with the wire whisk attachment (or using a hand mixer), whip the cream on medium-high speed until soft peaks form. Add the sugar and sambuca and continue to whip until stiff. Use immediately.

ASSEMBLE THE CUPCAKES

12. Fill a pastry bag with the espresso cream. Cut off the tip of the pastry bag to make a small opening. Insert the tip of the bag into the center of the cupcake and squeeze to release the filling. Repeat to fill all the cupcakes. Dip the tops of the cupcakes in the ganache. Fill another pastry bag fitted with a star tip, if desired, with the sambuca cream. Pipe a star of the cream onto the center of the cupcake. Top each with a chocolate-covered espresso bean.

Makes 18 standard-size cupcakes

Limoncello Cakes

Limoncello is the zesty lemon liqueur made in southern Italy where lemons are in abundance. The liqueur makes the cakes so flavorful, you might want to skip the filling.

Limoncello Curd Filling

4 extra-large egg yolks

$1/2$ cup granulated sugar

Finely grated zest of 2 lemons

8 tablespoons (1 stick) unsalted butter, cut into small pieces

2 tablespoons Limoncello

$1/4$ teaspoon salt

4 extra-large eggs, separated

$1/2$ pound (2 sticks) unsalted butter, softened

2 cups granulated sugar

Finely grated zest of 2 lemons

1 cup Limoncello

Cake

$2 1/2$ cups cake flour

2 teaspoons baking powder

Confectioners' sugar, for dusting

Candied lemon peel

MAKE THE FILLING

1. In a small saucepan, combine the egg yolks, granulated sugar, and zest. Heat over low heat, stirring constantly until thickened.

2. Remove from the heat. Stir in the butter and Limoncello. Pour the curd into a small bowl and cover the top with plastic wrap to prevent a skin from forming. Refrigerate overnight. (The curd can be made 2 or 3 days in advance.)

MAKE THE CAKE

3. Preheat the oven to 350°F. Line standard-size cupcake pans with paper liners.

4. Combine the cake flour, baking powder, and salt in a small bowl. Set aside.

5. In the bowl of a stand mixer fitted with the wire whisk attachment (or using a hand mixer), whip the egg whites until stiff. Set aside.

6. In another mixer bowl, using the paddle attachment (or using a hand mixer), cream the butter on medium-high speed. Add the granulated sugar gradually and beat on medium-high speed until light. Add the lemon zest and egg yolks with the mixer on low speed. Add the flour mixture to the egg mixture alternately with the Limoncello, starting and ending with the flour mixture, and mix until well blended.

7. Gently fold the egg whites into the mixture.

8. Spoon the batter into the lined cupcake pans.

9. Bake the cupcakes for 15 to 20 minutes, or until a cake tester inserted into the center comes out with a fine crumb.

10. Remove the pans from the oven. Cool the cupcakes in the pans on wire racks. Cool completely before filling.

ASSEMBLE THE CUPCAKES

11. Fill a pastry bag with the Limoncello curd. Cut off the tip of the pastry bag to make a small opening. Insert the tip of the bag into the middle of the cupcake and squeeze to release the filling. Repeat until all of the cupcakes are filled. Dust the tops with confectioners' sugar. Top each cupcake with a piece of candied lemon peel.

Makes 16 standard-size cupcakes

SMALL, SWEET, AND ITALIAN

INTELLIGENTI

Save the egg whites to bake a batch of Espresso Meringues (see page 124), Chocolate Cookie Cannoli (see page 54), "Ugly but Good" Chunky Chocolate-Hazelnut Meringues (*Brutti ma Buoni*) (see page 113), Angel Food Cupcakes (see page 34), or amaretti (see pages 117–122).

Fig and Rum Holiday Fruitcakes

Fruitcakes are an Italian Christmas tradition. This tasty version can be easily doubled and makes a great holiday gift, paired with a coffee shop gift card or a pound of quality coffee beans.

I've baked these in a 4-inch square cupcake pan just for an interesting change, but you can use jumbo round pans or mini loaf pans for a more traditional fruitcake presentation.

1 cup almonds, coarsely chopped

2 cups dried figs, coarsely chopped

$1/2$ cup dark rum

Grated zest of 1 orange

8 tablespoons (1 stick) unsalted butter, softened

1 cup sugar

2 extra-large eggs

$1^1/_2$ cups all-purpose flour

1 teaspoon baking powder

$1/4$ teaspoon salt

1. In a small bowl, combine the almonds, figs, rum, and orange zest. Cover and macerate at room temperature overnight.
2. Preheat the oven to 350°F. Line a jumbo-size cupcake pan with paper liners.
3. In the bowl of a stand mixer fitted with the paddle attachment (or using a hand mixer), cream the butter and sugar on medium-high speed until light. Add the eggs and mix until well blended.
4. With the mixer on low speed, gradually add the flour, baking powder, and salt and mix just until blended.

5. Stir in fig and rum mixture.
6. Fill the lined cupcake pan three-quarters full with the batter.
7. Bake the cupcakes 20 to 25 minutes, or until a cake tester inserted into the center comes out with a fine crumb.
8. Remove the pan from the oven. Let the cupcakes cool in the pan on a wire rack.

Makes 6 jumbo cupcakes

Mini Pumpkin Cakes

TORTINE DI ZUCCA

Nothing celebrates the fall season better than these mini, moist pumpkin cakes. They are simply topped with a swirl of vanilla mascarpone frosting and a sprinkle of cinnamon-sugar—seasonal and sensational.

Pumpkin Cupcakes

3 extra-large eggs

1¼ cups sugar

1½ cups canned pure pumpkin purée

1¼ cups vegetable oil

1½ cups all-purpose flour

1½ teaspoons baking powder

1½ teaspoons ground cinnamon

1 teaspoon salt

1 teaspoon baking soda

Vanilla Mascarpone Frosting

4 tablespoons (½ stick) unsalted butter, softened

½ cup mascarpone cheese

3 cups confectioners' sugar

1 teaspoon pure vanilla extract

Cinnamon-sugar (2 teaspoons ground cinnamon mixed with ¼ cup granulated sugar)

MAKE THE PUMPKIN CUPCAKES

1. Preheat the oven to 350°F. Line mini cupcake pans with paper liners.
2. In the bowl of a stand mixer fitted with the paddle attachment (or using a hand mixer), mix the eggs, sugar, pumpkin, and oil on medium-high speed until well blended.
3. With the mixer on low, add the flour, baking powder, cinnamon, salt, and baking soda and mix just until blended.

4. Fill the lined cupcake pans three-quarters full with the batter.

5. Bake the cupcakes for 15 to 20 minutes or until a cake tester inserted into the center comes out with a fine crumb.

6. Remove the pans from the oven. Transfer the cupcakes to wire racks to cool. Cool completely before frosting.

MAKE THE FROSTING

7. In the bowl of a stand mixer fitted with the paddle attachment (or using a hand mixer), cream the butter and mascarpone on low speed until smooth. Gradually add the confectioners' sugar and vanilla and beat on high speed for 5 to 8 minutes, or until very light and fluffy.

ASSEMBLE THE CUPCAKES

8. Fill a pastry bag with the frosting. Cut off the tip of the pastry bag to make a small opening. Pipe the frosting onto the tops of the cupcakes, starting at the outer edges and circling in to the centers. Sprinkle with the cinnamon-sugar.

Make 45 mini cupcakes

Angel Food Cupcakes

TORTINE D'ANGELI

*Lighter than heaven, or the angels in it, these little cakes are the perfect
treat when you want a little something sweet—and with less guilt. Enjoy
them plain, or top with seasonal fruit. For the fullest volume, be sure to
have your egg whites at room temperature before whipping.*

$\frac{1}{2}$ cup cake flour

Pinch of salt

$\frac{3}{4}$ cup sugar

5 egg whites, at room temperature

$\frac{1}{2}$ teaspoon cream of tartar

Seasonal fruit (optional)

1. Preheat the oven to 350°F. Line standard-size cupcake pans with paper liners.
2. In a small bowl, combine the cake flour, salt, and $\frac{1}{2}$ cup of the sugar. Set aside.
3. In the bowl of a stand mixer fitted with the wire whisk attachment (or using a hand mixer), beat the egg whites and cream of tartar on high speed until soft peaks form. With the mixer running, add the remaining $\frac{1}{4}$ cup sugar and beat until stiff.
4. Gently fold the flour mixture into the egg whites.
5. Fill the lined cupcake pans three-quarters full with the batter. Don't fill to the top; angel food cakes need room to grow as they bake.
6. Bake the cupcakes for 15 to 20 minutes, or until lightly browned and center springs back when touched.
7. Remove the pans from the oven. Let the cupcakes cool in the pans on wire racks. Serve at room temperature, plain or topped with seasonal fruit.

Makes 14 standard-size cupcakes

INTELLIGENTI

Save the egg yolks to make Limoncello curd (see page 27) or pastry cream.

Cassata Cupcakes

Traditional cassata from Sicily comes in many different forms: from fancy marzipan-topped bakery cassata to simple baked ricotta cakes made a casa. I like to bake an assortment of vanilla sponge and chocolate sponge cupcakes and top them with an assortment of ricotta, pretty pale green marzipan, and candied orange rind.

Sponge Cupcakes

4 extra-large eggs

1 cup granulated sugar

Pinch of salt

1¼ cups cake flour

Chocolate Sponge Cupcakes

4 extra-large eggs

1 cup granulated sugar

Pinch of salt

¾ cup cake flour

½ cup unsweetened Dutch-process
    cocoa powder

Ricotta Filling

2 cups ricotta cheese

1 cup confectioners' sugar

Finely grated zest and juice of
    1 orange

Frosting

Ricotta Filling and confectioners' sugar
    or
Pale green marzipan

Maraschino cherries and/or candied
    orange peel, for garnish

CANDIED CITRUS PEEL

2 oranges (or lemons)
1 cup water
1 cup sugar
Additional sugar, for coating

1. Remove the peel from the oranges (or lemons), and cut it into strips. Be sure to leave the pith attached to the peel. Place the peel in a medium saucepan, and add the water and sugar.
2. Bring to a boil. Reduce the heat to low and boil, without stirring, until reduced, about 20 minutes.
3. Using 2 forks, remove the peel from the pan and toss in the additional sugar. Set the peel on a parchment paper–lined baking sheet to cool and dry. The peel can be made 2 or 3 days in advance. Store, unwrapped, at cool room temperature.

MAKE THE SPONGE CUPCAKES

1. Preheat the oven to 350°F. Line standard-size cupcake pans with paper liners.
2. Combine the eggs, sugar, and salt in a stainless-steel bowl set over a saucepan of simmering water. Lightly whisk until the temperature of the mixture reaches 110°F. This will help add volume to your sponge.

3. Transfer the egg mixture to the bowl of a stand mixer fitted with the wire whisk attachment (or use a hand mixer), and whip on high speed until very light, pale, and thick, 10 to 12 minutes. I always set a timer for this stage because it is so important.

4. Fold in the flour (and cocoa if using), a quarter at a time, being careful not to deflate the foam.

5. Fill the lined cupcake pans two-thirds full with the batter.

6. Bake the cupcakes for 15 to 20 minutes, or until golden brown and center springs back when touched.

7. Remove the pans from the oven. Cool in pans before filling and frosting.

MAKE THE FILLING

8. In a medium bowl, combine all of the ingredients and mix with a wooden spoon or spatula until blended. Refrigerate until ready to use. (The filling can be made 1 day in advance.)

ASSEMBLE THE CUPCAKES

9. Fill a pastry bag with the ricotta filling. Cut off the tip of the pastry bag to make a small opening. Insert the tip of the bag into the center of the cupcake. Squeeze to release the filling. Repeat to fill all of the cupcakes.

10. Dust each cupcake with confectioners' sugar, top with a dollop of ricotta filling, and garnish with a maraschino cherry and/or candied orange peel.

11. Or for a marzipan topping, knead a drop or two of green food coloring into marzipan. On a surface lightly dusted with confectioners' sugar, roll the marzipan out into a thin layer. Using a fluted cookie cutter, cut the marzipan into 3-inch circles. Place a circle of marzipan on top of each cupcake. Use a bit of ricotta filling to adhere a maraschino cherry and/or candied orange peel to each cupcake. Refrigerate until serving.

Makes 12 to 15 standard-size cupcakes

Neopolitan Cupcakes

These three-layer strawberry cupcakes are inspired by the popular three-flavor ice cream and layered with chocolate and vanilla whipped cream. Topped with perfectly ripened strawberries, they are sure to impress even the most jaded cupcake fan.

Strawberry Cupcakes

$2\frac{1}{2}$ cups cake flour

3 teaspoons baking powder

$\frac{1}{4}$ teaspoon salt

$1\frac{1}{2}$ cups sugar

12 tablespoons ($1\frac{1}{2}$ sticks) unsalted butter, softened

5 extra-large egg whites

1 cup puréed strawberries

Chocolate Whipped Cream

$\frac{3}{4}$ cup heavy cream

6 tablespoons unsweetened Dutch-process cocoa powder

$\frac{1}{4}$ cup sugar

16 small, fresh strawberries, for topping

Whipped Cream

1 cup heavy cream

$\frac{1}{2}$ cup sugar

MAKE THE STRAWBERRY CUPCAKES

1. Preheat the oven to 350°F. Line standard-size cupcake pans with paper liners.

2. In the bowl of a stand mixer fitted with the paddle attachment (or using a

hand mixer), mix the flour, baking powder, salt, and sugar on low speed. Add the butter and mix until uniformly blended.

3. Add the egg whites and strawberry purée and mix on low speed for about 1 minute.

4. Scrape down the sides and bottom of the bowl. Beat on medium-high speed for 2 minutes, or until the batter is blended and smooth.

5. Fill the lined cupcake pans two-thirds full with the batter.

6. Bake the cupcakes for 20 to 25 minutes, or until a cake tester inserted into the center comes out with a fine crumb.

7. Remove the pans from the oven. Carefully remove the cupcakes from the pans and transfer to wire racks to cool. Cool completely before filling.

MAKE THE WHIPPED CREAM

8. In the bowl of a stand mixer fitted with the wire whisk attachment (or using a hand mixer), whip the cream on medium-high speed until soft peaks form. Add the sugar and beat on high speed until stiff. Use immediately.

MAKE THE CHOCOLATE WHIPPED CREAM

9. In the bowl of a stand mixer fitted with the wire whisk attachment (or using a hand mixer), whip the cream and cocoa on medium-high speed until soft peaks form. Add the sugar and beat on high speed until stiff. Use immediately.

ASSEMBLE THE CUPCAKES

10. Remove the cupcakes from the paper liners and discard the liners. Cut each cupcake into thirds horizontally. Place the tops of the cupcakes into fresh paper liners.

11. Fill a pastry bag with the chocolate whipped cream. Cut off the tip of the pastry bag to make a small opening. Squeeze the cream onto the bottoms of the cup-

cakes. Top with the middle layers. Fill a pastry bag with the plain whipped cream. Cut off the tip of the pastry bag to make a small opening. Squeeze the whipped cream onto the middle layers. Top with the remaining cupcake layers.

12. Pipe whipped cream on the tops of the cupcakes and garnish each with small, fresh strawberries. Refrigerate until serving.

Makes 16 standard-size cupcakes

Mini Christmas Panettone

These perfect personal-size panettone make an ideal Christmas morning breakfast in bed. If you have any leftovers, this panettone makes great French toast or bread pudding.

2 packages active dry yeast
   (4 teaspoons)
1 cup lukewarm water
8 tablespoons (1 stick) unsalted butter,
   melted and cooled
5 extra-large eggs
$1/2$ cup sugar

Finely grated zest of 2 lemons
5 to $5^1/2$ cups all-purpose flour
2 teaspoons salt
2 cups dried cranberries
1 cup sliced almonds

1. Line a standard-size cupcake pan with parchment paper. Cut the parchment paper to measure 1 inch above the sides of the pan to form a collar. Set aside.
2. In a small bowl, sprinkle the yeast over the lukewarm water. Set aside.
3. In the bowl of a stand mixer fitted with the paddle attachment (or using a hand mixer), combine the butter, 4 of the eggs, the sugar, and the zest. Mix until well blended. Gradually add 4 cups of the flour and the salt. Stir in the cranberries and almonds.
4. Turn the dough out onto a generously floured surface. Knead the dough, adding the remaining 1 to $1^1/2$ cups flour as needed to make a soft but not sticky dough.

5. Place the dough into a large buttered bowl, cover with plastic wrap, and let rise in a warm spot until doubled in bulk, 1 to 1½ hours. (I use the top of the stove for this when the oven is on.)

6. Turn the dough out onto a lightly floured surface. Knead into 12 smooth balls.

7. Place the dough balls into the lined cupcake pan. Cover with plastic wrap and let rise in the pan until doubled in bulk, 25 to 35 minutes.

8. Preheat the oven to 400°F.

9. Using a sharp knife or scissors, cut a cross on top of each panettone.

10. In a small bowl, beat the remaining 1 egg. Brush the tops of the panettone with the beaten egg. Bake the panettone for 25 to 30 minutes, or until golden brown and firm.

11. Cool the panettone in the pan.

12. Remove from the pan and remove and discard the parchment paper liners.

Makes 12 small panettone

Pistachio-Chocolate Cupcakes

These cupcakes combine two of my brother's favorite flavors, pistachio and chocolate. I try to bake them for him every birthday, one cupcake per year. Top generously with chocolate whipped cream and sprinkle with chopped pistachios for a tasty buon compleanno *celebration.*

Cupcakes

2 1/2 cups cake flour

1 teaspoon baking powder

1/4 teaspoon salt

1/2 pound (2 sticks) unsalted butter, softened

2 cups sugar

1 teaspoon pure vanilla extract

4 extra-large eggs

1 cup sour cream

1 cup unsalted pistachios, finely chopped, plus more for garnish

1/2 cup finely chopped semisweet chocolate, plus more for garnish

Chocolate Whipped Cream

2 cups heavy cream

1/2 cup unsweetened Dutch-process cocoa powder

1 cup sugar

MAKE THE CUPCAKES

1. Preheat the oven to 350°F. Line standard-size cupcake pans with paper liners.
2. In a small bowl, combine the flour, baking powder, and salt. Set aside.

3. In the bowl of a stand mixer fitted with the paddle attachment (or using a hand mixer), cream the butter and sugar on medium-high speed until light. Add the vanilla.

4. Add the eggs, one at a time, beating well after each addition.

5. With the mixer on low speed, add the flour mixture to the egg mixture alternately with the sour cream, beginning and ending with the flour mixture.

6. Stir in the pistachios and chocolate.

7. Fill the lined cupcake pans two-thirds full with the batter.

8. Bake the cupcakes for 15 to 20 minutes, or until a cake tester inserted into the center comes out with a fine crumb.

9. Remove the pans from the oven. Transfer the cupcakes to wire racks to cool. Cool completely before frosting and filling.

MAKE THE CHOCOLATE WHIPPED CREAM

10. In the bowl of a stand mixer fitted with the wire whisk attachment (or using a hand mixer), whip the cream and cocoa on medium-high speed until soft peaks form. Add the sugar and beat on high speed until stiff. Use immediately.

ASSEMBLE THE CUPCAKES

11. Fill a pastry bag with the chocolate whipped cream. Cut off the tip of the pastry bag to make a small opening. Insert the tip of the pastry bag into the center of the cupcake. Squeeze to release the filling. Repeat until all the cupcakes are filled. Pipe the remaining chocolate cream on top of the cupcakes and sprinkle with additional chopped pistachios and chocolate.

Makes 22 standard-size cupcakes

Toasted Almond Cupcakes

Old World flavors meet New World in our newest and most popular cupcake flavor. A tasty almond cake is filled with almond cream and topped with fluffy buttercream and crunchy amaretti and biscotti crumbs. To dress these cupcakes up, top with a pine nut flower.

Cupcakes

2 1/2 cups cake flour

3 teaspoons baking powder

1/4 teaspoon salt

1 1/2 cups granulated sugar

12 tablespoons (1 1/2 sticks) unsalted butter, softened

5 extra-large egg whites

1 cup whole milk

2 teaspoons pure almond extract

Almond Cream Filling

3/4 cup heavy cream

1/4 cup granulated sugar

1 teaspoon pure almond extract

Almond Buttercream Frosting

1/2 pound (2 sticks) unsalted butter, softened

6 cups confectioners' sugar

1/4 cup water, or more as needed

2 teaspoons pure almond extract

Topping

1 cup crushed amaretti and biscotti crumbs (see page xxi)

Pine nut flowers, for garnish (optional)

MAKE THE CUPCAKES

1. Preheat the oven to 350°F. Line standard cupcake pans with paper liners.
2. In the bowl of a stand mixer fitted with the paddle attachment (or using a hand mixer), mix the flour, baking powder, salt, and sugar on low speed. Add the butter and mix until uniformly blended.
3. Add the egg whites, milk, and almond extract and mix on low speed for about 1 minute.
4. Scrape down the sides and bottom of the bowl. Beat on medium-high speed for 2 minutes, or until the batter is blended and smooth.
5. Fill the lined cupcake pans two-thirds full with the batter.
6. Bake the cupcakes for 20 to 25 minutes, or until a cake tester inserted into the center comes out with a fine crumb.
7. Remove the pans from the oven. Carefully remove the cupcakes from the pans and transfer to wire racks to cool. Cool completely before filling.

MAKE THE FILLING

8. In the bowl of a stand mixer fitted with the wire whisk attachment (or using a hand mixer), whip the cream on medium-high speed until soft peaks form. Add the sugar and almond extract and beat on high speed until stiff. Use immediately.

MAKE THE FROSTING

9. In the bowl of a stand mixer fitted with the paddle attachment (or using a hand mixer), mix all of the ingredients on low speed until blended. Increase the speed to high and whip for 3 to 4 minutes, or until very fluffy. Use immediately.

ASSEMBLE THE CUPCAKES

10. Fill a pastry bag with the almond cream filling. Cut off the tip of the pastry bag to make a small opening. Insert the tip of the bag into the center of the cupcake and squeeze to release the filling. Repeat until all the cupcakes are filled.

11. Fill a pastry bag with the almond buttercream frosting. Cut off the tip of the pastry bag to make a small opening. Pipe the frosting onto the tops of the cupcakes, starting at the outer edges and circling in to the centers. Roll the outer edges of the cupcakes in amaretti and biscotti crumbs. Top each with a pine nut flower, if desired. Refrigerate until serving.

Makes 18 standard-size cupcakes

Italian Pastries

Many fancier Italian pastries are traditionally made in pastry shops. With a few tips, these recipes will have you baking pastries at home like a pro. Just be sure to read through all the components and directions before starting. Buona fortuna!

Traditional Sicilian Cannoli

Chocolate Cookie Cannoli with
    Whipped Cream

Cream Puffs with Strawberry
    Mascarpone Filling *(Bignè al Forno)*

Zeppole di San Giuseppe with Almond
    Ricotta Filling and Blackberry Sauce

Baby Rum Babas

Strawberry Napoleons *(Mille Foglie)*

Chocolate and Chestnut Calzones

Nick's Ricotta Zeppole

Apples in Pastry with Brandy Cream
    (Mele in Crosta)

Classic Pasticiotte

Pear and Date Nut Strudel

Italian Cream Horns

Sweet Popovers

Sweet Fried Risotto Balls
    (Arancine Dolci)

Crespelle with Whipped Cream and
    Orange-Caramel Sauce

Rum Squares

Pizzelle Cups with Ice Cream and Fresh
    Fruit

Nutella Banana Panini

Traditional Sicilian Cannoli

Although I love creating new and interesting twists on most classic pastries, I must admit I am a cannoli snob—or purist, I like to think. Why tamper with perfection? Nothing beats a crispy, just-fried shell filled with a sweet pistachio-and-chocolate-studded ricotta filling and a simple dusting of confectioners' sugar. These can be tricky to make, especially if the weather is humid; it makes the dough more elastic. The key is to just enjoy the process. If your shells come out less-than-perfect, I call that home style. If you want perfection, buy machine-made shells.

The newest trend for cannoli is Cannoli Stacks or Cannoli Chips and Dip. For the stacks, simply fry the rounds flat, not wrapped around a cannoli tube. After cooling, layer with cannoli filling like a napoleon. For Chips and Dip, fry rounds flat, cool them, and serve with a bowl of ricotta filling for dipping.

Instead of the ¾ cup all-purpose flour and ¾ cup cake flour, you can use 1 ½ cups "00" flour.

Shells

¾ cup all-purpose flour

¾ cup cake flour

2 tablespoons sugar

Pinch of salt

1 teaspoon unsweetened Dutch-process
    cocoa powder

2 tablespoons cold unsalted butter

½ cup Marsala wine

Egg white, for sealing

Oil, for frying

Filling

4 cups ricotta cheese, drained overnight

1 cup confectioners' sugar

½ cup chopped pistachios

½ cup chopped chocolate chips

½ teaspoon finely grated lemon zest

Confectioners' sugar, for dusting

MAKE THE SHELLS

1. In a food processor, combine the flours, sugar, salt, and cocoa and pulse until blended. Add the butter and pulse until blended. Add the Marsala and pulse to make a soft dough. Turn the dough out onto a lightly floured surface and knead until smooth and elastic, 5 to 7 minutes. Form the dough into a ball, wrap in plastic wrap, and let rest at room temperature for 1 hour.

2. Roll the out dough to a thickness of ⅛ inch. Cut into 4-inch rounds. (If making Cannoli Stacks or Chips, cut the dough into 3-inch rounds.) Keep the dough covered with plastic wrap until ready to wrap and fry. Wrap each dough circle around a cannoli tube that has been lightly sprayed with nonstick cooking spray. Seal the edges with egg white.

3. In a medium saucepan over moderate heat, heat the oil to 350°F. Fry the shells, two or three at a time, until golden brown. Using tongs, carefully remove the tubes from the oil and transfer to paper towels to drain. Let cool.

4. Carefully twist the tubes to remove the shells from the tubes. Let the tubes cool completely before rewrapping with the remaining dough circles. (For Cannoli Stacks or Chips, prick the dough with a fork. Fry two or three at a time, until light brown. Transfer to paper towels to drain.) Let cool before assembling.

MAKE THE FILLING

5. In a bowl, combine all of the ingredients and mix well. Place the filling in a pastry bag. Cut off the tip of the pastry bag to make a small opening. Squeeze the filling into both ends of the shells. Sprinkle the ends with additional pistachios and dust with confectioners' sugar, if desired. Refrigerate until serving.

Makes about 20 cannoli

CANNOLI TIPS

- The dough can be made 1 day ahead. Wrap in plastic wrap and refrigerate overnight. Let the dough come to room temperature before frying.
- The shells can be fried 1 day in advance. Store the shells in an airtight container at room temperature.
- Draining the ricotta overnight will help reduce excess moisture and will ensure that your filling is not runny. Place the ricotta in a fine-mesh sieve set over a bowl, cover, and refrigerate overnight.
- Don't fill the cannoli shells until you are almost ready to serve. Filling them too early will make them soggy. The ideal cannoli has a crispy shell.

Chocolate Cookie Cannoli with Whipped Cream

These light and crispy chocolate cookies are baked and then formed into shells. Dip the ends of the shells in melted chocolate and fill with fresh whipped cream for a delicious variation on traditional cannoli. Even a cannoli purist like me can love this version, because it's chocolate.

Shells

9 tablespoons (1 stick plus 1 tablespoon) unsalted butter, softened

1 cup confectioners' sugar

1 cup all-purpose flour

$\frac{1}{4}$ cup unsweeted Dutch-process cocoa powder

Pinch of salt

4 extra-large egg whites

1 teaspoon pure vanilla extract

4 ounces semisweet chocolate, melted

Filling

1 cup heavy cream

3 tablespoons sugar

Confectioners' sugar, for garnish

MAKE THE SHELLS

1. Preheat the oven to 350°F. Line baking sheets with parchment paper.
2. In the bowl of a stand mixer fitted with the paddle attachment (or using a hand mixer), cream the butter and confectioners' sugar on medium-high speed. Add the flour, cocoa, and salt and mix on low speed just until the mixture resembles

coarse crumbs. Add the egg whites and vanilla and mix on medium-high speed until smooth.

3. Drop the batter from a tablespoon onto the prepared pan, spacing the cookies about 6 inches apart. Using a small offset spatula dipped in water, spread the dough into thin circles with a 5-inch diameter.

4. Bake the cookies for about 8 minutes, or until firm.

5. Remove the pan from the oven. Quickly and carefully roll the hot cookies onto cannoli tubes. Place them seam sides down on the lined baking sheet. Let cool completely on the tubes. Carefully twist to remove the shells from the tubes.

6. In a bowl set over simmering water or using the microwave, melt chocolate. Dip the ends of the cooled cannoli shells into melted chocolate. Set aside on parchment paper to dry.

MAKE THE FILLING

7. In the bowl of a stand mixer fitted with the wire whisk attachment (or using a hand mixer), whip the heavy cream on high speed until soft peaks form. Add the sugar and beat until stiff. Fill a pastry bag with the whipped cream. Cut off the tip of the pastry bag to make a small opening. Squeeze the filling into both ends of the shells. Dust the tops lightly with confectioners' sugar. Serve immediately.

Makes about 20 cannoli

Cream Puffs with Strawberry-Mascarpone Filling

BIGNÈ AL FORNO

The pasta bignè *used in this recipe and for zeppole is a classic building block of pastry. It is a tried-and-true component that I've taught and enjoyed over the years. The flexibility is what makes it ideal. Fill with whipped cream, Chocolate Whipped Cream, or pastry cream, your choice. Or try this delicious variation of strawberry-mascarpone filling, a new flavor and a new classic.*

Cream Puffs

8 tablespoons (1 stick) unsalted butter

1 cup water

Pinch of salt

1 cup all-purpose flour

4 extra-large eggs, at room temperature

Strawberry-Mascarpone Filling

1 pound mascarpone cheese

1 cup granulated sugar

2 cups frozen strawberries, thawed and slightly drained

Confectioners' sugar, for dusting

MAKE THE CREAM PUFFS

1. Preheat the oven to 375°F. Line baking sheets with parchment paper.
2. In a medium saucepan over medium-high heat, combine the butter, water, and salt and bring to a boil. Add the flour quickly, all at once, and stir with a wooden spoon until the mixture pulls away from the sides of the pan and a film forms on the bottom of the pan, about 3 minutes.

3. Remove the pan from the heat. Spoon the mixture into the bowl of a stand mixer fitted with the paddle attachment (or use a hand mixer). On medium high speed, add the eggs, one at a time, mixing well after each addition. Mix well to achieve a smooth, sticky dough. Fill a pastry bag with the dough. Pipe 2-inch rounds (or spoon out rounds with a teaspoon) onto the lined baking sheets, spacing them about 1 inch apart.

4. Bake the puffs for 25 to 30 minutes, or until golden brown.

5. Remove the baking sheets from the oven. Cool the puffs on the sheets or on wire racks. Let cool completely before filling. The puffs can be made 1 to 2 days in advance and stored at room temperature. They can also be frozen for up to one week. If they are in an airtight container, they will lose their crispness. So, to re-crisp (even after thawing), place them onto a parchment-lined cookie sheet and bake at 350°F for 5 minutes. Cool, then fill.

MAKE THE FILLING

6. Combine all of the ingredients in a small bowl and mix until blended. Use immediately.

ASSEMBLE THE CREAM PUFFS

7. Cut the puffs in half horizontally. Fill a pastry bag with the strawberry-mascarpone filling. Cut off the tip of the pastry bag to make a small opening. Pipe the filling onto the bottom halves of the puffs. Top with the other halves of the puffs. Dust with confectioners' sugar. Refrigerate until serving.

Makes about 30 cream puffs

Zeppole di San Giuseppe with Almond-Ricotta Filling and Blackberry Sauce

Zeppole are traditionally made for the feast day of San Giuseppe, March 19. These fried puffs are traditionally filled with vanilla pastry cream and topped with a dusting of confectioners' sugar and a maraschino cherry, but almond-ricotta filling and blackberry sauce are just as tasty. Use a square of oiled parchment paper to slip the zeppole into the hot oil. It makes frying these much easier and helps keep the size consistent. Zeppole are best when fried, filled, and enjoyed on the same day.

Zeppole

8 tablespoons (1 stick) unsalted butter

1 cup water

Pinch of salt

1 cup all-purpose flour

4 extra-large eggs, at room temperature

Almond-Ricotta Filling

2 cups ricotta cheese

1 cup confectioners' sugar

$1/2$ teaspoon pure almond extract

Blackberry Sauce

3 cups frozen blackberries, thawed

1 cup granulated sugar

2 tablespoons red wine

Vegetable oil, for frying

Confectioners' sugar, for dusting

MAKE THE ZEPPOLE

1. Cut parchment paper into ten 2-inch squares. Lightly oil the squares with vegetable oil and set aside.

2. In a medium saucepan over medium-high heat, combine the butter, water, and salt and bring to a boil. Add the flour quickly, all at once, and stir with a wooden spoon until the mixture pulls away from the sides of the pan and a film forms on the bottom of the pan, about 3 minutes.

3. Remove the pan from the heat. Spoon the mixture into the bowl of a stand mixer fitted with the paddle attachment (or use a hand mixer). Add the eggs, one at a time, mixing well after each addition on medium-high speed. Mix well to achieve a smooth, sticky dough.

4. In a medium saucepan over moderate heat, heat the oil to 350°F.

5. Fill a pastry bag fitted with the star tip with the dough. Pipe the dough onto a piece of oiled parchment paper. Slip the dough into the hot oil and fry until golden. Be sure to keep frying when the dough puffs up and splits. You want to be sure it cooks inside.

6. Using a slotted spoon, remove the zeppole from the oil and transfer to paper towels to drain. Repeat to make all the zeppole.

MAKE THE FILLING

7. In a bowl, combine all of the ingredients and mix well. Use immediately or store, refrigerated, in an airtight container. (The filling can be made 1 day in advance.)

8. Place the filling into a pastry bag. Cut off the tip of the pastry bag to make a small opening. Insert the tip of the pastry bag into the bottom of a zeppole. Squeeze to release the filling. Repeat until all the zeppole are filled.

9. Dust the tops with confectioners' sugar and serve with blackberry sauce.

MAKE THE SAUCE

10. In a food processor, pulse the blackberries, granulated sugar, and wine until smooth, then strain. Use immediately or refrigerate for 3 to 4 days.

Makes about 25 zeppole

Baby Rum Babas

These traditional tiny brioches are soaked in a rich rum syrup, brushed with apricot glaze, and sprinkled with a healthy dose of grated orange zest. An Old World tradition, revisited, resized, slightly updated, but still delicious. For the fullest flavor, be sure to soak the babas when they are slightly warm.

Rum Syrup

1 cup sugar

1 cup water

$1/2$ cup dark rum

4 extra-large eggs

8 tablespoons (1 stick) unsalted butter,
    softened

Babas

$1/4$ cup sugar

$1/2$ cup warm whole milk

1 package active dry yeast
    (2 teaspoons)

2 cups cake flour

1 teaspoon salt

Glaze (optional)

Apricot preserves

Finely grated orange zest

MAKE THE RUM SYRUP

1. In a medium saucepan over medium heat, bring the sugar and water to a boil. Boil for 3 to 4 minutes or until the sugar has dissolved.

2. Remove from the heat and stir in the rum.

MAKE THE BABAS

3. In a small bowl, combine 2 tablespoons of the sugar, the milk, and the yeast. Set aside to proof.

4. In the bowl of a stand mixer fitted with the wire whisk attachment (or using a hand mixer), combine the flour, salt, and remaining 2 tablespoons sugar. Mix on low speed. Add the yeast mixture and mix until blended.

5. With the mixer on medium speed, add the eggs, one at a time, beating well after each addition.

6. Gradually mix in the softened butter, 1 tablespoon at a time. The mixture should be smooth and similar to pancake batter.

7. Cover and place in a warm space. Let rise until almost doubled, about 30 minutes.

8. Preheat the oven to 400°F. Grease and flour or spray mini cupcake pans with nonstick cooking spray.

9. Fill the prepared cupcake pans about three-quarters full with the batter. Cover and let rise until the batter reaches the top of the pans, 20 to 30 minutes.

10. Bake the babas for 15 to 20 minutes, or until golden brown and cake tester inserted into the center comes out clean.

11. Remove the pans from the oven. Let the babas cool slightly in the pans before removing. Carefully remove and add the babas to the rum syrup. Let soak for 15 to 20 minutes.

GLAZE THE BABAS (OPTIONAL)

12. In a small pan, heat the preserves over low heat. Strain the warm preserves. Brush the babas with the glaze and sprinkle with the orange zest.

Makes 36 rum babas

Strawberry Napoleons

MILLE FOGLIE

These flaky layers of puff pastry are sandwiched with vanilla pastry cream and fresh sliced strawberries: a dressed-up strawberry shortcake. Get creative and layer them with any farm-fresh berries, whipped cream, or ricotta filling.

Pastry

1 sheet frozen puff pastry, thawed according to manufacturer's directions

1 egg, lightly beaten

Vanilla Pastry Cream

1 cup whole milk

$1/2$ cup granulated sugar

$1/4$ cup cornstarch

3 extra-large egg yolks

1 teaspoon pure vanilla extract

8 tablespoons ($1/2$ stick) unsalted butter, cut into 4 pieces

$1^{1}/_{2}$ cups fresh sliced strawberries

Confectioners' sugar, for dusting

MAKE THE PASTRY

1. Preheat the oven to 400°F.
2. Place the thawed puff pastry on a parchment paper–lined baking sheet. Prick it with a fork and brush with beaten egg. Cut the pastry into 2-inch squares.
3. Bake the squares until golden brown, about 20 minutes, pricking the pastry every 5 minutes to keep it flat.
4. Remove the pan from the oven. Set aside to cool completely before filling.

(*On large plate, clockwise from top center*) Chocolate-Cherry Amaretti, Pistachio Butter Cookies, Nutella Thumbprints, Sicilian Fig Cookies (*Cuccidati*); (*plate on right*) "Ugly but Good" Chunky Chocolate-Hazelnut Meringues (*Brutti ma Buoni*); (*plate on bottom left*) Pumpkin Biscottini (*Biscottini di Zucca*)

Mini Christmas Panettone

Cream Puffs with Strawberry-Mascarpone Filling (*Bignè al Forno*)

(*Top plate, left to right*) Godfather Cupcakes, Neopolitan Cupcakes, Toasted Almond Cupcakes

(*Clockwise from upper left*) Cassata Cupcakes, Sweet Popovers, Neopolitan Wheat Pies (*Pastiera*), Classic Pasticiotte, Lemon-Almond Amaretti

Zeppole di San Giuseppe

(*Clockwise from upper left*) Rum Squares, Traditional Sicilian Cannoli, Baby Rum Babas

(*Left to right*) "Ugly but Good" Chunky Chocolate-Hazelnut Meringues (*Brutti ma Buoni*) with Cherry-Vanilla Semifreddo with Chocolate Sauce, Mocha Chip Biscottini with Chocolate-Espresso Pudding with Sambuca Cream (*Budino di Ciccolato*), Buttermilk Panna Cotta with Crushed Amaretti and Berries

MAKE THE PASTRY CREAM

5. In a medium saucepan over low heat, bring ½ cup of milk and ¼ cup sugar just to a boil. In a mixing bowl, combine the cornstarch, egg yolks, the remaining ¼ cup sugar, and the remaining ½ cup milk.

6. Slowly whisk hot milk mixture into egg mixture in a thin stream. Return the mixture to the pan and whisk constantly until boiling and thick. Remove from heat, then stir in the butter and vanilla.

7. Transfer to a small bowl and place a piece of plastic wrap directly on the surface to prevent a skin forming on top. Cool completely before using. (The pastry cream can be made 1 to 3 days in advance. Store in an airtight container in the refrigerator.)

ASSEMBLE THE NAPOLEONS

8. Spoon the pastry cream onto one-half of the pastry squares. Top each with a few slices of strawberries. Place the remaining pastry squares on top to form sandwiches. Dust the tops with confectioners' sugar and garnish each with a strawberry slice.

9. Place the napoleons in paper liners, if desired. Serve immediately or refrigerate until serving time. Napoleons are best served on same day they are made; otherwise the pastry will be soggy.

Makes 20 napoleons

Chocolate and Chestnut Calzones

One of my first foodie memories was learning how chestnuts grow, three in a pod. I was with my mom at her friend's house and literally got hit in the head with a falling chestnut. Chestnut has been a favorite flavor ever since, especially when paired with chocolate. Making these mini turnovers is a great way to use up leftover chestnuts.

Crust

1$\frac{1}{2}$ to 2 cups all-purpose flour

Pinch of salt

8 tablespoons (1 stick) unsalted butter

$\frac{1}{2}$ cup sour cream

$\frac{1}{2}$ cup semisweet chocolate chips

$\frac{1}{4}$ cup honey

2 tablespoons fig jam

1 tablespoon Marsala wine

Filling

1$\frac{1}{2}$ cups roasted chestnuts, coarsely chopped

1 egg, lightly beaten

MAKE THE CRUST

1. In a food processor, combine 1½ cups of the flour and the salt. Add the butter and pulse until uniform. Add the sour cream. Turn the dough out onto a lightly floured surface and knead to make a soft, not sticky, dough, adding the remaining ½ cup flour as needed. Wrap the dough in plastic wrap and refrigerate for 2 to 3 hours or overnight.

MAKE THE FILLING

2. Preheat the oven to 350°F. Line baking sheets with parchment paper. In a small bowl, combine the chestnuts, chocolate chips, honey, jam, and Marsala and stir to combine.

3. Remove half of the dough from the refrigerator. On a lightly floured surface, roll the dough out to a thickness of ⅛ inch. Cut into 3-inch rounds. Place approximately ½ teaspoon of the filling into the center of each round. Brush the outer edges of the dough with beaten egg.

4. Fold the dough over the filling and press the edges to seal. Place the calzones on the lined baking sheets, spacing them 2 inches apart. Brush the tops with the beaten egg.

5. Repeat with other half of the dough and remaining filling.

6. Bake the calzones for 15 to 20 minutes, or until golden brown.

7. Remove the pans from the oven. Cool the calzones on the pans. Serve warm or at room temperature.

Makes about 36 mini calzones

ROASTING CHESTNUTS

To roast chestnuts: Use a paring knife to make a slit against the grain of the shell. Place into a shallow baking dish and roast in the oven at 400°F. for about 25 minutes. Chestnuts are much easier to peel when they are warm.

Nick's Ricotta Zeppole

These light ricotta fritters are a delicious staple of Italian pastry, perfected by my friend Chef Nick Mancini of La Tavola Ristorante. Simply dust with confectioners' sugar and dip them into a rich chocolate-espresso sauce.

Zeppole

2 extra-large eggs

2 tablespoons granulated sugar

1¼ cups ricotta cheese

¾ cup whole milk

½ teaspoon pure vanilla extract

¼ teaspoon freshly grated
   nutmeg

½ teaspoon finely grated lemon
   zest

1½ cups all-purpose flour

4 teaspoons baking powder

¼ teaspoon salt

Canola oil, for frying

Confectioners' sugar, for dusting

Chocolate-Espresso Dipping Sauce

1 cup bittersweet chocolate, melted

½ cup heavy cream

1 shot espresso

MAKE THE ZEPPOLE

1. In the bowl of a stand mixer fitted with the paddle attachment (or using a hand mixer), combine the eggs, granulated sugar, cheese, milk, vanilla, nutmeg, and lemon zest and mix on medium speed until well blended. Add the flour, baking powder, and salt and mix the batter until smooth.

2. Cover the bowl with plastic wrap and refrigerate the batter for at least 3 hours or overnight.

3. In a medium saucepan over medium heat, heat the oil to 350°F.

4. From a teaspoon measure, carefully drop the batter into the hot oil. Fry the zeppole until golden brown, turning them so all sides cook. Remove the zeppoles from the hot oil with a slotted spoon and transfer to paper towels to drain. Dust with confectioners' sugar and serve with the dipping sauce.

MAKE THE SAUCE

5. Melt the chocolate in a stainless-steel bowl set over a saucepan of simmering water, or in the microwave. Stir in the heavy cream and espresso and mix until blended. Use immediately or store, refrigerated, in an airtight container. (The sauce can be made 3 or 4 days in advance. Gently reheat when needed.)

Makes 30 zeppole

Apples in Pastry with Brandy Cream

MELE IN CROSTA

> *One of the best ways to enjoy nature's best, wrapped in pastry. Use what-ever firm, flavorful apple variety is in season. The firmness of Golden Delicious works great, or a tart Braeburn or Granny Smith. Whenever I teach this in pastry class people are always amazed at its simplicity. Another great dessert to wow your friends.*

1 sheet frozen puff pastry, thawed according to manufacturer's directions

2 apples, peeled, cored, and halved

1/4 cup apricot preserves

2 teaspoons ground cinnamon

1/4 cup sugar

Egg wash (see page xviii)

Brandy Whipped Cream

1 cup heavy cream

1/4 cup sugar

1/4 cup brandy

WRAP THE APPLES

1. Preheat the oven to 400°F. Line a baking sheet with parchment paper.
2. On a lightly floured surface, roll out the pastry to a thickness of 1/8 inch. Cut into four equal pieces.
3. Brush the apple halves with apricot preserves. Sprinkle with some of the cinnamon and sugar. Wrap each apple half in a piece of pastry and place, seam sides down, on sheet.

4. Brush the pastry with egg wash and sprinkle with more of the cinnamon and sugar. For a more decorative look, re-roll pastry scraps and cut it into a leaf shape or other desired shape. Adhere the shapes to the pastry with egg wash.
5. Bake the pastry-wrapped apples for 20 to 25 minutes, or until golden brown.
6. Remove the baking sheet from the oven. Let the apples cool slightly.

MAKE THE BRANDY WHIPPED CREAM

7. In the bowl of a stand mixer fitted with the wire whisk attachment (or using a hand mixer), whip the cream on medium-high speed until soft peaks form. Add the sugar and whip on high speed until stiff. Stir in the brandy. Use immediately.
8. Plate the apples individually and serve warm with a dollop of brandy cream on each one.

Makes 4 apples in pastry

Classic Pasticiotte

This classic double-crust pie is simply filled with vanilla pastry cream. Many bakeries use ricotta filling or chocolate pastry cream, but I prefer this traditional vanilla version. It was always my dad's favorite, so I stick with it.

There are several components to this dessert. Think ahead and make the crust and pastry cream one day ahead, then assemble the tiny pies the next day.

Crust *(Pasta Frolla)*

2 cups all-purpose flour, plus
    more as needed

1/2 cup sugar

1/4 teaspoon salt

8 tablespoons (1 stick) cold
    unsalted butter

2 extra-large eggs

2 tablespoons cold water

1/4 cup cornstarch

3 extra-large egg yolks

1 teaspoon pure vanilla extract

4 tablespoons (1/2 stick) unsalted
    butter, cut into 4 pieces

Egg wash (see page xviii)

Pastry Cream

1 cup whole milk

1/2 cup sugar

MAKE THE CRUST

1. In a food processor, combine the flour, sugar, and salt and pulse until blended. Add the butter and pulse until the mixture is crumbly. Add the eggs and water

and mix until blended. Turn the dough out onto a lightly floured surface and knead in any additional flour to make a soft, nonsticky dough. Wrap the dough in plastic and refrigerate for 2 hours or overnight.

MAKE THE PASTRY CREAM

2. In a medium saucepan over low heat, bring ½ cup milk and ¼ cup sugar just to a boil. In a mixing bowl, whisk the egg yolks, cornstarch, remaining ¼ cup sugar, and remaining ½ cup milk.

3. Slowly whisk hot milk mixture into egg mixture in a thin stream. Return the mixture to the pan and whisk constantly over low heat until boiling and thick. Remove from heat, then stir in the butter and vanilla.

4. Transfer to a small bowl and place a piece of plastic wrap directly on the surface to prevent a skin forming on top. Cool completely before using. (The pastry cream can be made 1 to 3 days in advance. Store in an airtight container in the refrigerator.)

ASSEMBLE THE PASTICIOTTE

5. Preheat the oven to 350°F.

6. On a lightly floured surface, roll out the dough to a thickness of ⅛ inch. Cut into 4-inch rounds. Press the rounds into mini pie pans with a 2¼-inch diameter.

7. Fill each pie with the pastry cream. Brush the edges of the crusts with egg wash. Top each with another circle of dough. Press the edges together to seal. Be sure to pinch the seams well and pinch the crust edges up, as opposed to over the pans. This will make it easier to remove them from the pans after baking.

8. Brush the tops with egg wash.

9. Bake the pasticiotte for 20 to 25 minutes, or until golden brown.

10. Remove the pans from the oven. Cool the pasticiotte in pans on a wire rack. When cool, carefully remove from the pans.

Makes 12 pasticiotte

Pear and Date Nut Strudel

When I was growing up, pears were always in abundance thanks to Grandpa Ralph, who planted our backyard tree. During the harvest, we enjoyed pears as dessert along with mixed nuts and cheese, or in desserts like this easy-to-make strudel. These strudel slices are a snap to make using store-bought puff pastry.

Filling

2 cups diced pears

1 cup dates, coarsely chopped

$1/4$ cup sugar

1 teaspoon ground cinnamon

$1/2$ cup walnuts, coarsely chopped

Crust

1 sheet frozen puff pastry, thawed according to manufacturer's directions

1 egg, slightly beaten

Additional cinnamon and sugar, for sprinkling

1. Preheat the oven to 400°F. Line a baking sheet with parchment paper.
2. In a food processor, combine all of the filling ingredients and pulse until blended.
3. On a lightly floured surface, roll out the dough to a thickness of $1/8$ inch. Cut the pastry in half lengthwise into two pieces approximately 14 × 6 inches. Place half of the filling in the center of each strip of dough, brush each end with beaten egg, and roll the dough up jelly-roll-style. Press to seal and place, seam sides down, on the lined baking sheet.
4. Brush the tops with beaten egg and sprinkle with cinnamon and sugar.
5. Bake the strudel for 20 to 25 minutes, or until golden brown.

6. Remove the pan from the oven. Let the strudel cool on the baking sheet.

7. Transfer the strudel to a cutting board and cut, diagonally, into 1-inch slices. Place the slices in paper liners, and serve.

Makes about 20 pieces

Italian Cream Horns

Baking these cream-filled shells is an easy way to impress people and another way to use those metal cannoli tubes. To avoid soggy shells, be sure to fill them right before serving. Fill with your choice of whipped cream, pastry cream, or ricotta cream. My favorite filling is this version of chocolate whipped cream with a touch of amaretto.

Shells

1 package puff pastry, thawed according to manufacturer's directions

Egg wash (see page xviii)

$1/4$ cup granulated sugar

2 tablespoons amaretto

Confectioners' sugar, for dusting

Filling

1 cup heavy cream

$1/4$ cup unsweetened Dutch-process cocoa powder

MAKE THE SHELLS

1. Preheat the oven to 375°F. Line a baking sheet with parchment paper.
2. Lightly spray metal cannoli tubes with nonstick cooking spray.
3. On a lightly floured surface, roll out the sheet of pastry to a thickness of $1/8$ inch and prick all over with a fork.
4. Using a pastry cutter, cut the pastry into strips measuring approximately $1/2$ inch wide × 6 inches long.

5. Roll the strips of pastry onto the cannoli tubes, slightly overlapping to form a 3-inch-long shell. You can fit 2 shells rolled onto the ends of each cannoli tube. Place the tubes, seam sides down, onto the lined baking sheet. Brush with egg wash.
6. Bake the shells for 12 to 15 minutes, or until golden brown.
7. Remove the baking sheet from the oven. Let the shells cool on the cannoli tubes. When cool, carefully hold each shell and twist the tube to release the shell.

MAKE THE FILLING

8. In the bowl of a stand mixer fitted with the wire whisk attachment (or using a hand mixer), whip the cream and cocoa on medium-high speed until soft peaks form. Add the granulated sugar and amaretto and whip on high speed until stiff. Use immediately.

ASSEMBLE THE CREAM HORNS

9. Fill a pastry bag with the chocolate whipped cream. Cut off the tip of the pastry bag to make a small opening. Pipe the cream into each end of each shell. Dust the tops with confectioners' sugar.

Makes 16 cream horns

Sweet Popovers

This is an updated version of my mother-in-law's recipe. She shares her secret to these light and crispy treats: "Keep the ingredients at room temperature, whip the eggs and oil well, and be sure to bake until golden brown to avoid soggy centers." A generous drizzle of lemon confectioners' icing tops these puffs beautifully.

Popovers

2 cups all-purpose flour

1 teaspoon baking powder

9 extra-large eggs, at room temperature

1 cup vegetable oil

1 teaspoon pure vanilla extract

Lemon Confectioners' Icing

3 cups confectioners' sugar

$\frac{1}{4}$ cup water

1 teaspoon lemon extract

MAKE THE POPOVERS

1. Preheat the oven to 400°F. Grease and flour or spray mini muffin pans with non-stick cooking spray.

2. In a small bowl, combine the flour and baking powder.

3. In the bowl of a stand mixer fitted with the wire whisk attachment (or using a hand mixer), beat the eggs and oil on high speed for 5 minutes. Add the vanilla and mix to incorporate.

4. With the mixer on low speed, gradually add the flour mixture. Then beat on high speed for 5 minutes more.

5. Spoon the batter into the prepared pans, filling each cup three-quarters full with the batter.

6. Bake the popovers for 20 to 25 minutes, or until golden brown.

7. Remove the pans from the oven. Cool the popovers in the pans on wire racks. Remove from the pans and continue to cool completely on the wire racks.

MAKE THE ICING

8. In the bowl of a stand mixer fitted with the paddle attachment (or using a hand mixer), beat all of the icing ingredients until smooth. (The icing can be made 2 days in advance. Refrigerate in an airtight container. Let come to room temperature and remix before using.)

9. Place the wire racks with the popovers onto a parchment paper–lined baking sheet. Drizzle the icing over the popovers. Let dry at room temperature.

Makes 36 popovers

Sweet Fried Risotto Balls

ARANCINE DOLCI

A sweet inspiration from the savory meat-filled Sicilian arancine. These rice pudding fritters have a crispy outer shell and a creamy gooey center. Be sure to cook most of the liquid out of the rice pudding before rolling, freezing, and frying these treats. They are so good on their own, no dipping sauce is needed.

$1/2$ cup Arborio rice

1 cup whole milk

$1/4$ cup sugar

$1/4$ cup heavy cream

$1/4$ cup semisweet chocolate chips

Canola oil, for frying

1 egg, slightly beaten

1 cup biscotti crumbs, finely ground
   (see page xxi)

1. In a small saucepan, combine the rice, milk, sugar, and heavy cream and bring to a gentle boil over low heat. Reduce the heat to a simmer and cook, stirring often, until the rice is al dente and almost all the liquid has evaporated, 25 to 30 minutes. Set aside to cool. Cover and refrigerate overnight.

2. Roll the rice pudding into 1-inch balls, inserting 3 or 4 chocolate chips into the center of each one. Freeze the balls for 1 hour or overnight.

3. Using a deep-fryer or heavy-gauge skillet over medium heat, heat 3 inches of oil to 375°F.

4. Roll the rice balls in the beaten egg, then coat with the biscotti crumbs.

5. Fry the rice balls, three or four at a time, until golden brown, turning as needed. Using a slotted spoon, remove from the oil and transfer to paper towels to drain.

6. Serve immediately.

Makes 12 to 15 sweet rice balls

Crespelle with Whipped Cream and Orange-Caramel Sauce

Light and delicate little stacks of crepes are layered with whipped cream and a subtle orange-caramel sauce. Be sure the crepes are thin and don't stress about the shape of the crepes; home style is fine. Plate the crepes in stacks of four and serve.

Orange-Caramel Sauce

1/2 cup sugar

3 tablespoons water

1 tablespoon corn syrup

1 tablespoon butter

1/2 cup heavy cream

Finely grated zest of 1 orange

1/2 cup buttermilk

1/2 cup all-purpose flour

1/4 teaspoon salt

Whipped Cream

1/2 cup heavy cream

1/4 cup sugar

Crepes

1 extra-large egg

1 tablespoon butter, melted and cooled

MAKE THE SAUCE

1. In a small saucepan over medium heat, combine the sugar, water, and corn syrup and bring to a boil. Let boil, without stirring, until the mixture is a deep amber color. Remove from the heat and add the butter, heavy cream, and orange zest and stir until blended.

2. Pour the caramel into a small bowl and cover the top directly with plastic wrap to prevent a skin forming. Refrigerate for 2 to 3 hours or overnight. (The sauce can be made 2 or 3 days in advance.)

MAKE THE CREPES

3. In a small bowl, whisk the egg. Add the butter, buttermilk, flour, and salt. Mix until the batter is smooth. Cover and refrigerate 30 minutes. (The crepe batter can be made 1 day in advance.)

4. Heat a small nonstick skillet or crepe pan over medium-low heat. Drop a teaspoon of batter into the skillet. Smooth and spread the batter on the bottom of the skillet with the back of the spoon.

5. Cook until golden brown, 1 to 2 minutes. Using a nonstick spatula, flip and cook the opposite side of the crepe for 1 to 2 minutes, until golden.

6. Transfer the cooked crepe to a platter. Repeat cooking crepes with the remaining batter.

MAKE THE WHIPPED CREAM

7. In the bowl of a stand mixer fitted with the wire whisk attachment (or using a hand mixer), beat the cream on medium-high speed until soft peaks form. Add the sugar and continue to beat on high speed until stiff. Use immediately.

ASSEMBLE THE CREPES

8. Place one crepe on a serving dish and spread with a thin layer of whipped cream. Continue to layer crepes and cream to make 6 stacks of 4 crepes each, ending with a crepe on top.

9. Gently warm the caramel sauce over low heat and drizzle it over the stacks of crepes just before serving.

Makes 6 crepe stacks

Rum Squares

These pastries are the blueprint for the classic Italian rum cake. As a child it wasn't my favorite, but now I savor every morsel of the rum-soaked sponge cake, sandwiched with vanilla and chocolate pastry cream and puff pastry. Be sure to use a serrated knife in a sawing motion to cut these into squares.

Sponge Cake

4 extra-large eggs

1 cup sugar

Pinch of salt

$1\frac{1}{4}$ cups cake flour

6 extra-large egg yolks

2 teaspoons pure vanilla
  extract

8 tablespoons (1 stick) unsalted butter,
  cut into 8 pieces

$\frac{1}{4}$ cup coarsely chopped semisweet
  chocolate, for the Chocolate Pastry
  Cream

Pastry

2 sheets frozen puff pastry, thawed
  according to manufacturer's directions

Egg wash (see page xviii)

Pastry Cream

2 cups whole milk

$\frac{3}{4}$ cup sugar

$\frac{1}{2}$ cup cornstarch

Rum Syrup

1 cup sugar

1 cup water

$\frac{1}{2}$ cup dark rum

MAKE THE SPONGE CAKE

1. Preheat the oven to 350°F. Line an 11 × 9-inch quarter-sheet pan with parchment paper.

2. Combine the eggs, sugar, and salt in a stainless-steel bowl set over a saucepan of simmering water. Lightly whisk until the temperature of the mixture reaches 110°F. This will help add volume to your sponge.

3. Transfer the egg mixture to the bowl of a stand mixer fitted with the wire whisk attachment (or use a hand mixer), and whip on high speed until very light, pale, and thick, 10 to 12 minutes. I always set a timer for this stage because it is so important.

4. Carefully fold in flour, a quarter at a time, being careful not to deflate the foam.

5. Spread the batter into the prepared pan.

6. Bake the cake for 15 to 20 minutes, or until golden brown and the center springs back when touched.

7. Remove the pan from the oven. Cool the cake in the pan completely before assembling. (The cake can be made and frozen 2 weeks in advance. Thaw before assembly.)

BAKE THE PASTRY

8. Preheat the oven to 400°F.

9. Place the puff pastry sheets on a parchment paper–lined baking sheet. Prick the pastry with a fork and brush with egg wash.

10. Bake the pastry for 15 to 20 minutes, or until golden brown, pricking the pastry with a fork every 5 minutes. This will keep the pastry flat.

MAKE THE PASTRY CREAM

11. In a medium saucepan over low heat, bring 1 cup milk and ½ cup sugar just to a boil. In a mixing bowl, whisk cornstarch, egg yolks, remaining ¼ cup sugar, and remaining 1 cup milk.

12. Slowly whisk hot milk mixture into egg mixture in a thin stream. Return the mixture to the pan and whisk constantly over low heat until boiling and thick. Remove from the heat and stir in the vanilla and butter.

13. Transfer half the mixture to a small bowl and place a piece of plastic wrap directly on the surface to prevent a skin from forming on top. Cool completely before using.

14. Add the chocolate to the remaining half of the mixture and stir until the chocolate has melted and the mixture is smooth. Transfer to a small bowl and place a piece of plastic wrap directly on the surface to prevent a skin from forming on top. Cool completely before using. (The pastry cream can be made 1 to 3 days in advance. Place in an airtight container and refrigerate.)

MAKE THE RUM SYRUP

15. In a medium saucepan over medium heat, bring the sugar and water to a boil. Boil until the sugar has dissolved, 3 to 4 minutes. Remove from the heat and stir in the rum.

ASSEMBLE THE RUM SQUARES

16. Spread the chocolate pastry cream over one layer of puff pastry. Top with the layer of sponge cake. Brush and soak the sponge cake with rum syrup. Spread a layer of vanilla pastry cream on top of the sponge cake and top with the remaining layer of puff pastry. Refrigerate for 2 to 3 hours or overnight. Slice into 2-inch squares with a serrated knife. Place in paper liners, if desired.

Makes about 25 squares

Pizzelle Cups with Ice Cream and Fresh Fruit

These thin and crispy waffles have a subtle anise flavor that pairs well with almost any combination of ice cream and fresh fruit. While the pizzelles are hot, carefully form each one into a cup by pressing it into a ramekin. When it cools, you'll have an Italian waffle cup. Perfect as a part of a create-your-own gelato sundae bar.

2 cups all-purpose flour

2 teaspoons baking powder

Pinch of salt

3 extra-large eggs

1 cup sugar

$1/2$ teaspoon anise oil

8 tablespoons (1 stick) unsalted butter, melted and cooled

Ice cream and fresh fruit, for serving

1. Preheat a pizzelle iron according to the manufacturer's directions.
2. In a small bowl, combine the flour, baking powder, and salt.
3. In the bowl of a stand mixer fitted with the paddle attachment (or using a hand mixer), beat the eggs and sugar on medium speed. Add the anise oil and melted butter and mix until blended.
4. With the mixer on low speed, gradually add the flour mixture and mix to make a sticky dough.
5. Drop the dough from a teaspoon onto the hot iron, close, and bake the pizzelle until golden brown, 40 to 50 seconds.
6. Carefully remove the pizzelle. While hot, carefully press each pizzelle into a ramekin to form a cup.
7. Cool completely before filling.
8. Fill with ice cream and fruit, as desired.

Makes about 20 to 24 pizzelle cups

Nutella Banana Panini

This sweet and gooey sandwich is delicious combination of Nutella and bananas. Press it as you would a savory panini, cut into quarters, and serve warm.

4 thick slices bread, such as challah

6 ounces Nutella hazelnut spread

2 bananas, cut in half lengthwise

4 tablespoons ($\frac{1}{2}$ stick) unsalted
  butter

Coarse sugar, for sprinkling

Confectioners' sugar, for dusting
  (optional)

Ice cream, for serving
  (optional)

1. Preheat a panini grill to medium heat. (Or heat a medium skillet over medium heat on the stovetop.)
2. Spread the hazelnut spread over 2 slices of bread. Place sliced bananas on top of the hazelnut spread. Press the other 2 slices of bread on top of the banana to form sandwiches. Spread butter on each side of the sandwiches and sprinkle with a generous amount of coarse sugar.
3. Place each sandwich on the preheated panini grill. Press down the top of the grill.
4. Cut each sandwich into 4 pieces. Dust with confectioners' sugar, if desired. Serve warm, with ice cream, if desired.

Makes 8 pieces

Pies and Tarts

Small pies and tarts always catch my eye when I walk past any pastry shop in Italy. Fruit filled, lattice topped, or simply glazed, they are sure to satisfy any sweet tooth. Pasta Frolla is the traditional Italian pie crust, simply made in a food processor. It can be made 2 to 3 days in advance and kept fresh by wrapping in plastic wrap and refrigerating. Or double wrap the dough and freeze for 1 to 2 weeks.

Many of these pies and tarts have components, especially the Easter Wheat Pies. Read the recipe a few times and try to prep some of the components in advance of assembly. Mangia dolci.

Neopolitan Wheat Pies

PASTIERA

This traditional pie made to celebrate Easter has a lot of delicious components. Each family from the Naples region has their own closely guarded recipe. My family always baked this version that includes pastry cream. As a result, the filling is much creamier and richer than most.

My mom would bake this pie the night before Easter (in a much bigger portion) and I'd fall asleep with the sweet smell of spring from the orange flower water–scented pie.

Crust

2 cups all-purpose flour, plus more as needed

1/2 cup sugar

1/4 teaspoon salt

8 tablespoons (1 stick) cold unsalted butter

2 extra-large eggs

2 tablespoons cold water

Egg wash (see page xviii)

Wheat

3 cups water

1/2 teaspoon salt

1 cup wheat berries or barley

Pastry Cream

3 extra-large egg yolks

1/2 cup sugar

1 tablespoon cornstarch

1 cup whole milk

Ricotta Filling

4 extra-large eggs

3/4 cup sugar

2 cups ricotta cheese

1 teaspoon orange flower water

Finely grated zest of 2 oranges

Finely grated zest of 2 lemons

MAKE THE CRUST

1. In a food processor, combine the flour, sugar, and salt and pulse until blended. Add the butter and pulse until the mixture is crumbly. Add the eggs and water and mix until blended. Turn the dough out onto a lightly floured surface and knead in additional flour, as needed, to make a soft, nonsticky dough. Wrap the dough in plastic wrap and refrigerate for 2 hours or overnight. (The dough can be made 1 to 2 days in advance or frozen for 1 week in advance.)

COOK THE WHEAT

2. In a small saucepan, bring the water and salt to a boil. Add the wheat berries or barley, cover, reduce the heat to low, and simmer until al dente, about 45 minutes. You don't want to overcook the wheat at this stage, otherwise it will be mushy in the pie. Drain, set aside, or refrigerate overnight.

MAKE THE PASTRY CREAM

3. In a small saucepan over low heat, combine all of ingredients and cook, whisking constantly, until thickened. Pour into a bowl and place a piece of plastic wrap directly on the surface to prevent a skin from forming. Set aside or refrigerate until you are ready to assemble the pies.

MAKE THE FILLING

4. In a small bowl, beat together the eggs and sugar. Add the ricotta, orange flower water, and orange and lemon zests and mix until smooth.

ASSEMBLE THE PIES

5. Combine the pastry cream, ricotta filling, and wheat and stir until blended.
6. Preheat the oven to 350°F.
7. On a lightly floured surface, roll out the dough to a thickness of ⅛ inch. Cut the dough into 4-inch rounds. Press the rounds into small 2½-inch pie pans.

8. Fill the crusts with the filling.

9. Roll out the remaining dough to a thickness of ⅛ inch. Using a pastry cutter, cut the dough into ¼-inch-wide strips. Lay the strips over the filling in a lattice pattern. Be sure to press the ends of the strips to the edges of the crusts to adhere. Place the pie pans on a sturdy baking sheet. Brush the tops of the pies lightly with egg wash.

10. Bake the pies for 25 to 30 minutes, or until the centers are just about set.

11. Remove the pies from the oven and transfer to a wire rack to cool.

12. Carefully remove the pies from the pans. Refrigerate until serving.

Makes twenty-four 2½-inch pies

Pear Crostata

These free-form, rustic pies are my favorite type of pie to make. Simply roll out the crust, cut it into circles, and fill the centers with lightly spiced fruit and a sprinkle of crushed amaretti. Roll the edges over, no fussy pie dishes or crimping necessary. This tart is the perfect example of baking locally—our own pears, backyard to table.

Crust

1 cup all-purpose flour

$\frac{1}{4}$ cup sugar

Pinch of salt

4 tablespoons ($\frac{1}{2}$ stick) cold unsalted
   butter

1 extra-large egg

1 tablespoon cold water

Filling

4 or 5 pears

$\frac{1}{4}$ cup sugar

2 teaspoons ground
   cinnamon

$\frac{1}{2}$ cup crushed amaretti
   cookies (optional)
   (see page xxi)

MAKE THE CRUST

1. In a food processor, combine the flour, sugar, and salt and pulse until blended. Add the butter and pulse until the mixture is crumbly. Add the egg and water and mix until blended. Turn the dough out onto a lightly floured surface and knead in additional flour, as needed, to make a soft, nonsticky dough. Wrap the dough in plastic wrap and refrigerate for 2 hours or overnight. (The dough can be made 2 to 3 days in advance or frozen for 1 week in advance.)

MAKE THE FILLING

2. Peel, core, and slice the pears. In a small bowl, combine the sugar and cinnamon. Set aside.

ASSEMBLE THE CROSTATAS

3. Preheat the oven to 350°F. Line a baking sheet with parchment paper.
4. Roll out the dough on a lightly floured surface to a thickness of ⅛ inch. Using a 6-inch cutter, cut the dough into rounds. Gather and re-roll the scraps as needed.
5. Place the rounds on the lined sheet, spacing them about 3 inches apart. Place some of the fruit in the center of each dough circle. Sprinkle with the cinnamon and sugar. Sprinkle with crushed amaretti, if using. Fold the edges of the dough up and slightly over the fruit to form an outer crust.
6. Bake the tarts for 15 to 20 minutes, or until golden brown.
7. Remove the pan from the oven and let the tarts cool on the pan for about 10 minutes. Using a spatula, carefully remove the tarts from the pan.
8. Serve warm or at room temperature.

Makes 6 crostatas

Blood Orange–Mascarpone Tarts

The bold citrus flavor of these red-fleshed oranges and the tender pastry crust combine to make these tarts a favorite summer dessert. The crust is so easy. No fussy rolling, just press the dough into tart pans.

Blood Orange Swirl

$1/2$ cup blood orange purée

1 tablespoon cornstarch

6 tablespoons ($3/4$ stick)
    unsalted butter, softened

1 extra-large egg yolk

Crust

$1/2$ cup confectioners' sugar

Pinch of salt

$3/4$ cup all-purpose flour, plus
    more as needed

Filling

$1^1/2$ cups mascarpone cheese

1 extra-large egg yolk

$1/2$ cup granulated sugar

MAKE THE BLOOD ORANGE SWIRL

1. In a small saucepan, heat the blood orange purée and cornstarch over low heat, whisking constantly, until thickened. Remove from the heat and set aside until cool.

MAKE THE CRUST

2. Preheat the oven to 350°F.

3. In a food processor, combine the confectioners' sugar, salt, and flour and pulse until blended. Add the butter and egg yolk and pulse to make a soft dough. If the dough is sticky, add a bit more flour.

4. Divide the dough into 4 equal pieces. Press the crust into the sides and bottoms of four 4-inch rectangular tart pans with removable bottoms. Line the crusts with aluminum foil and fill with pie weights or dried beans. Place the tart pans on a sturdy baking sheet.

5. Bake the tart shells for 10 to 12 minutes. Remove the pie weights or beans and the foil. Return the tart shells to the oven and bake for 5 minutes more.

6. Remove the tart shells from the oven. Transfer to a wire rack to cool.

MAKE THE FILLING

7. In the bowl of a stand mixer fitted with the paddle attachment (or using a hand mixer), combine the mascarpone, egg yolk, and granulated sugar. Beat on medium speed until smooth. Swirl the blood orange mixture into the mascarpone mixture and mix slightly just to marble.

ASSEMBLE THE TARTS

8. Pour the cooled filling into the prepared crusts.

9. Bake the tarts for 15 to 20 minutes or until just about set in the middle.

10. Remove the tarts from the oven. Transfer to wire racks to cool completely. Carefully remove the tarts from the tart pans.

Makes four 4-inch tarts

Torta Marmellata

These lattice-topped baked fruit tarts are available in most pastry shops across Italy. They are delicious filled with a seasonal variety of fruit. You can use your choice of premade pie filling or try my grandmother's New World favorite, blueberry.

Filling

1$\frac{1}{2}$ cups raspberry or apricot pie filling, or blueberry filling (see below)

Blueberry Filling

1$\frac{1}{2}$ pints fresh blueberries

$\frac{1}{2}$ cup sugar

1$\frac{1}{2}$ tablespoons cornstarch

$\frac{1}{2}$ cup water

2 teaspoons finely grated lemon zest

Crust

1 cup all-purpose flour

$\frac{1}{4}$ cup sugar

Pinch of salt

4 tablespoons ($\frac{1}{2}$ stick) cold unsalted butter

1 extra-large egg

1 tablespoon cold water

Whipped cream or ice cream (optional)

MAKE THE BLUEBERRY FILLING (IF USING)

1. In a medium saucepan over medium heat, combine the blueberries, sugar, cornstarch, and water. Bring to a boil and stir until thickened. Remove the pan from the heat.

2. Stir in the lemon zest. Cool before using. (The filling can be made 1 to 2 days in advance. Store refrigerated, in an airtight container.)

MAKE THE CRUST

3. In a food processor, combine the flour, sugar, and salt and pulse until blended. Add the butter and pulse until the mixture is crumbly. Add the egg and water and mix until blended. Turn the dough out onto a lightly floured surface and knead in additional flour, as needed, to make a soft, nonsticky dough. Wrap the dough in plastic wrap and refrigerate for 2 hours or overnight. (The dough can be made 2 to 3 days in advance or frozen for 1 week in advance.)

4. Preheat the oven to 350°F.

5. On a lightly floured surface, roll out the dough to a thickness of ⅛ inch. Using a 6-inch cutter, cut the dough into 6-inch rounds. Press the dough into the bottoms and up the sides of 4-inch tart pans with removable bottoms. Fill with the pie filling.

6. Roll out the remaining crust dough. Using a pastry cutter, cut the dough into ¼ × 4-inch strips. Lay the strips of dough over the filling in a crisscross pattern. Press the ends of the strips to attach them to the edges of the tart crusts.

7. Place the tarts on a sturdy baking sheet.

8. Bake the tarts for 20 to 25 minutes, or until lightly browned.

9. Remove the tarts from the oven. Transfer to a wire rack to cool.

10. Carefully remove the tarts from the pans. Serve at room temperature with a dollop of whipped cream or scoop of ice cream, as desired.

Makes 4 tarts

Nonna's Cinnamon Rice Pies*

This version of my grandmother's crustless rice pie is simply baked in ramekins for smaller individual servings. At Sweet Maria's we still bake a larger version at Easter, keeping the tradition alive. Grandma Mary's tip: "Be sure to cook the rice just until al dente. It will continue to bake in the pie and you don't want it to be mushy."

4 cups water

1/2 cup long grain white rice

4 extra-large eggs

1/2 cup sugar

2 teaspoons pure vanilla extract

2 cups ricotta cheese

1 cup whole milk

2 teaspoons ground cinnamon

1. In a medium saucepan over medium heat, bring the water to a boil. Add the rice. Reduce the heat to low and cook until the rice is al dente, 15 to 20 minutes.
2. Remove the rice from the heat, drain, and set aside to cool.
3. Preheat the oven to 375°F.
4. In the bowl of a stand mixer fitted with the paddle attachment (or using a hand mixer), beat the eggs on medium-high speed. Add the sugar and vanilla and mix to incorporate. Add the ricotta and mix until smooth.
5. Stir in the cooled rice and milk. Place eight ½-cup ramekins on a sturdy baking sheet. Pour the mixture into the ramekins. Sprinkle cinnamon on top of the rice mixture. Carefully place the baking sheet into the oven.
6. Bake the pies for 25 to 30 minutes, or until the center of the pie is just about set.

7. Remove from the oven. Transfer the ramekins to a wire rack to cool. Refrigerate until serving.

Makes eight ¹/₂-cup rice pies

*Wheat-free

Zia Ann's Chocolate Ricotta Pies

TORTA DI RICOTTA E CIOCCOLATI

I've always loved this chocolate-speckled ricotta pie that my husband's aunt Ann baked every Easter. It's hard to improve on her traditional recipe, but I've traded her crust for this rich chocolate version. It's never too much chocolate!

Crust

3/4 cup all-purpose flour

1/2 cup unsweetened Dutch-process
     cocoa powder

2 tablespoons sugar

1/2 teaspoon baking powder

Pinch of salt

4 tablespoons (1/2 stick) unsalted butter,
     softened

1 extra-large egg

Filling

2 extra-large eggs

1 1/2 cups ricotta cheese

1/2 cup sugar

2 ounces semisweet dark chocolate,
     coarsely chopped

MAKE THE CRUST

1. In a food processor, combine the flour, cocoa, sugar, baking powder, and salt and pulse until blended. Add the butter and pulse until uniform in texture. Add the egg and mix until blended. Wrap the dough in plastic wrap and set aside.

2. Preheat the oven to 350°F.

MAKE THE FILLING

3. In the bowl of a stand mixer fitted with the paddle attachment (or using a hand mixer), combine the eggs, ricotta, and sugar and mix on medium speed until blended. Stir in the chocolate.

ASSEMBLE THE PIES

4. On a lightly floured surface, roll out the dough to a thickness of ⅛ inch. Cut the dough into twelve 4-inch rounds. Press into small, 2½-inch-diameter pie pans. Place the pie pans on a sturdy baking sheet. Fill the crusts with the filling.
5. Bake the pies for 25 to 30 minutes, or until the centers of the pies are set.
6. Turn off the oven and let the pies cool gradually in the oven for 10 to 15 minutes. Remove the baking sheet from the oven and continue to cool on a wire rack. Remove the pies from the pans.
7. Serve at room temperature, or refrigerate overnight.

Makes twelve 2½-inch pies

Almond Blackberry Tarts

CROSTATA DI MANDORLE E MORE

These tarts filled with blackberries and frangipani *originated in Venice, but different versions of them can be found all over Italy. Each region bakes these with the ripest fruit available. They are as delicious as they are striking. A simple brush of egg wash gives them a professional shine.*

Crust

1 cup all-purpose flour, plus more as needed

$1/4$ cup sugar

Pinch of salt

4 tablespoons ($1/2$ stick) cold unsalted butter

1 extra-large egg

1 tablespoon cold water

$3/4$ cup sugar

2 extra-large eggs

1 cup all-purpose flour

$1^1/2$ cups blackberries (fresh or unthawed frozen)

Egg wash (see page xviii)

Filling

8 tablespoons (1 stick) unsalted butter, softened

8 ounces almond paste (or apricot kernel paste) broken into pebble-size pieces

MAKE THE CRUST

1. Preheat the oven to 350°F.

2. In a food processor, combine flour, sugar, and salt and pulse until blended. Add the butter and pulse until the mixture is crumbly. Add the egg and water and mix until blended. Turn the dough out onto a lightly floured surface and knead in additional flour, as needed, to make a soft, nonsticky dough. Wrap the dough in plastic wrap and refrigerate for 2 hours or overnight. (The dough can be made 1 to 2 days in advance or frozen for 1 week in advance.)

MAKE THE FILLING

3. In the bowl of a stand mixer fitted with the paddle attachment (or using a hand mixer), cream the butter and almond paste on medium speed until smooth. Add the sugar, eggs, and flour and beat until smooth. Stir in the blackberries.

ASSEMBLE THE TARTS

4. On a lightly floured surface, roll out the crust to a thickness of ⅛ inch. Cut the dough into fourteen 4-inch circles.

5. Press the dough circles into small, 2½-inch-diameter pie pans. Place the pie pans on a sturdy baking sheet.

6. Fill the crusts with the filling. Brush the tops with egg wash.

7. Bake the tarts for 25 to 30 minutes, or until golden brown.

8. Remove the baking sheet from the oven. Cool the tarts on the sheet on a wire rack.

9. Serve at room temperature.

Makes fourteen 2½-inch tarts

Nut Tarts

CROSTATA DI NOCI

These little tarts have a buttery crust and a rich filling of mixed nuts. You can use whatever nuts you prefer, but I like this combination of walnuts, almonds, and hazelnuts. The nuts roast as these tiny tarts bake. A brush of slightly warmed apricot preserves after baking gives them a shiny professional bakery look, plus another layer of flavor.

Crust

1 cup all-purpose flour

$\frac{1}{4}$ cup sugar

Pinch of salt

4 tablespoons ($\frac{1}{2}$ stick) cold unsalted butter

1 large egg

1 tablespoon cold water

Filling

1 cup sugar

3 extra-large eggs

$\frac{1}{2}$ cup corn syrup

3 tablespoons unsalted butter, melted and cooled

$\frac{1}{2}$ cup amaretto

2 cups mixed nuts (whole almonds, hazelnuts, and walnuts)

Glaze

3 tablespoons apricot preserves

MAKE THE CRUST

1. In a food processor, combine the flour, sugar, and salt and pulse until blended. Add the butter and pulse until the mixture is crumbly. Add the egg and water

and mix until blended. Turn the dough out onto a lightly floured surface and knead in additional flour, as needed, to make a soft, nonsticky dough. Wrap the dough in plastic wrap and refrigerate for 2 hours or overnight. (The dough can be made 2 days in advance or frozen for 1 week in advance.)

MAKE THE FILLING

2. In a medium bowl, combine the sugar, eggs, corn syrup, butter, and amaretto and whisk by hand until well blended. Stir in the nuts.

ASSEMBLE THE TARTS

3. Preheat the oven to 350°F.
4. On a lightly floured surface, roll out the dough to a thickness of 1/8 inch. Cut the dough into fourteen 4-inch circles. Press the dough into small, 2½-inch-diameter pie pans with a ¼-cup capacity. Place the pie pans on a sturdy baking sheet.
5. Fill the crusts with the filling.
6. Bake the tarts for 20 to 25 minutes, or until the centers of the tarts are set.
7. Remove the tarts from the oven and transfer to a wire rack to cool. Carefully remove the tarts from the pans.
8. In a small saucepan over low heat, warm the apricot preserves for 5 to 8 minutes. Brush the tops of the tarts with preserves.
9. Refrigerate the tarts until serving.

Makes fourteen 2½-inch tarts

Plum and Polenta Crisps with Honey and Greek Yogurt

A dollop of thick yogurt and an ample drizzle of honey accent these crumbly cornmeal crisps. Use plums or whatever fruit (apples, pears, berries) you prefer. Your choice of honey can also vary. Local and organic options are plentiful and many Italian brands offer chestnut or orange honey. Why not host a honey tasting party alongside these mini crisps?

Filling

6 plums, peeled, pitted, and sliced

$1/4$ cup sugar

$1/4$ cup red wine

$1/2$ cup sugar

$1/4$ teaspoon salt

8 tablespoons (1 stick) unsalted butter, softened

Crust

$1/4$ cup all-purpose flour

$3/4$ cup cornmeal

Vanilla-flavored Greek yogurt

$1/2$ cup honey

1. Preheat the oven to 350°F.
2. In a small bowl, combine the plums, sugar, and wine and set aside.
3. In the bowl of a stand mixer fitted with the paddle attachment (or using a hand mixer), combine the flour, cornmeal, sugar, and salt and mix on low speed until blended. Add the butter and mix on low speed until blended, but still slightly crumbly.

4. Spray eight ½-cup ramekins with nonstick cooking spray. Press half of the crumb mixture into the bottoms of the ramekins. Top with the plums. Press the remaining crumb mixture on top. Put the ramekins on a sturdy baking sheet.

5. Bake the crisps for 25 to 30 minutes, or until golden brown.

6. Remove the crisps from the oven. Transfer to a wire rack to cool.

7. Serve the crisps warm with a scoop of vanilla yogurt and a drizzle of honey for each.

Makes 8 crisps

Cookies

Italians are well known for their elaborate cookie trays. An assortment makes any event a special occasion. Cookies are naturally single-serve desserts, the perfect two or three bites to satisfy your sweet tooth.

Tutti Bene!

Double Chocolate Milanos

"Ugly but Good" Chunky Chocolate-Hazelnut Meringues *(Brutti ma Buoni)*

Spumoni Cookies

Lemon-Almond Amaretti

Raspberry-Almond Amaretti

Coffee-Almond Amaretti

Chocolate-Cherry Amaretti

Pistachio Butter Cookies

Espresso Meringues

Apricot-Walnut Biscottini

Mocha Chip Biscottini

Raspberry Biscottini with Chocolate Drizzle

Pumpkin Biscottini *(Biscottini di Zucca)*

Double Chocolate–Almond Biscottini

Nutella Thumbprints

Sicilian Fig Cookies *(Cuccidati)*

Cinnamon-Walnut Florentines

Polenta Cookies

Susan's Taralles

Brown Sugar Pizzelles

Double Chocolate Milanos

This classic factory-made cookie favorite gets a home-style twist with a double dose of chocolate. It's a thin chocolate cookie sandwiched with more chocolate. Be sure to pipe these cookies as evenly sized as possible. This will make it easier to pair and sandwich them.

1/2 pound (2 sticks) unsalted butter, softened

3/4 cup sugar

1 extra-large egg

1 cup all-purpose flour

1/2 cup unsweetened Dutch-process cocoa powder

Pinch of salt

1 cup semisweet chocolate chips

MAKE THE COOKIES

1. Preheat the oven to 350°F. Line baking sheets with parchment paper.
2. In the bowl of a stand mixer fitted with the paddle attachment (or using a hand mixer), cream the butter and sugar on medium-high speed until light. Add the egg and mix until well blended.
3. With the mixer on low speed, gradually add the flour, cocoa, and salt and mix just until blended.
4. Fill a pastry bag with the cookie dough. Cut off the tip of the pastry bag to make a small opening. Pipe the dough in rounds the size of nickels onto a lined baking sheet, spacing them about 2 inches apart.
5. Bake the cookies for 10 to 12 minutes. The cookies will be flat.
6. Remove the pan from the oven. Let the cookies cool on the baking sheet.

7. In a double boiler or in a stainless-steel bowl set over a saucepan of simmering water, or in the microwave, melt the chocolate chips.

ASSEMBLE THE COOKIES

8. Spread a bit of chocolate onto half of the cookies. Top with the remaining cookie halves.

Makes about 20 cookies

"Ugly but Good" Chunky Chocolate-Hazelnut Meringues*

BRUTTI MA BUONI

My friend Sally shared this family recipe years ago and it continues to be one of my favorites. It's best mixed old-style with a wooden spoon. She also shared these tips: "Be sure to not chop the nuts too much, just a few pulses. The large chunky hazelnuts give these cookies their character. Add egg whites, as needed. If the dough is too wet, the cookies will spread too much. Don't overbake them, and cool on parchment paper."

2 cups hazelnuts

1½ cups confectioners' sugar

2 tablespoons unsweetened
    Dutch-process cocoa powder

½ teaspoon ground cinnamon

1 to 2 egg whites

1. Preheat the oven to 400°F. Line baking sheets with parchment paper.
2. Place the hazelnuts on a lined baking sheet. Roast them for 15 to 20 minutes. Remove the nuts from the oven and place them in a clean kitchen towel. Roll the towel back and forth on a hard surface to release the skins from the nuts. Discard the skins. In a food processor, pulse the nuts a few times until very coarsely chopped.
3. Reduce the oven temperature to 350°F.
4. In a medium bowl, combine the confectioners' sugar, cocoa, and cinnamon and mix with a wooden spoon until blended. Add the hazelnuts and stir until distributed.

5. Add 1 egg white and stir to moisten the mixture; it will be thick and hard to stir. If there is not enough moisture to hold the mixture together, add more egg white, a tablespoon at a time, until the mixture is moistened, but not runny.

6. Drop teaspoons of the dough onto a parchment-lined baking sheet, spacing each 2 inches apart.

7. Bake the meringues for 12 to 15 minutes, or until firm.

8. Remove the pan from the oven. Let the meringues cool on the parchment paper on the pan. Store at room temperature in an airtight container.

Makes about 40 meringues

*Wheat-free

Spumoni Cookies

These are easy-to-make, slice-and-bake refrigerator cookies. Like the Italian flag, and the famous ice cream, these cookies feature a delicious trio of red, white, and green—cherry, vanilla, and pistachio. The color is subtle, so if you'd like more, just knead in a bit of red food coloring into the cherry dough and a bit of green food coloring into the pistachio dough.

12 tablespoons (1$\frac{1}{2}$ sticks) unsalted butter, softened

1 cup sugar

1 extra-large egg

1 teaspoon pure vanilla extract

2 cups all-purpose flour, plus more as needed

$\frac{1}{2}$ teaspoon baking powder

$\frac{1}{4}$ teaspoon salt

$\frac{1}{2}$ cup maraschino cherries, finely chopped

$\frac{1}{2}$ teaspoon cherry extract

$\frac{1}{2}$ cup pistachio paste

1. In the bowl of a stand mixer fitted with the paddle attachment (or using a hand mixer), cream the butter and sugar on medium-high speed until light. Add the egg and vanilla and mix until well blended.
2. With the mixer on low speed, add the flour, baking powder, and salt and mix until well blended to form a soft dough.
3. Divide the dough into thirds.
4. Knead the cherries and cherry extract into one-third of the dough. Add additional flour as you knead to make the dough less sticky.
5. Knead the pistachio paste into another third, kneading in some additional flour to make the dough less sticky.

6. Roll each piece of dough into a cylinder, about 24 inches long. Cut each cylinder in half. Press one plain cylinder on top of one cherry cylinder and top with a green cylinder, to form a red, white, and green striped pattern. Press them together and flatten the top slightly. Repeat with the remaining dough cylinders.

7. Wrap the dough in plastic wrap and refrigerate overnight. (The dough can be refrigerated for 2 to 3 days in advance or frozen for 1 to 2 weeks.)

8. Preheat the oven to 350°F. Line a baking sheet with parchment paper.

9. Using a sharp, straight knife, slice the striped dough into ¼-inch slices and place them on the lined baking sheet, spacing them 2 inches apart.

10. Bake the cookies for 10 to 12 minutes, or until the edges are lightly browned.

11. Remove the pan from the oven. Transfer the cookies to a wire rack to cool. Store at room temperature in an airtight container.

Makes 40 cookies

ALL ABOUT AMARETTI

Amaretti are the backbone of Italian cookies. These flavorful macaroons are made from almond paste or apricot kernel paste.

Almond paste is made from grinding blanched almonds and sugar. Apricot kernel paste is made from grinding apricot kernels with sugar. It is generally more flavorful than almond paste.

Be careful when purchasing; it's expensive and many store-bought brands can contain too much sugar and not enough almonds and/or apricot kernels. Too much sugar will ruin your dough and make your cookies runny and flat. (See "Ingredients," page 166.)

Naturally wheat-free and gluten-free, amaretti are simply made by mixing the paste, sugar, and egg whites, plus optional flavoring, just until blended. A tiny dot of food coloring makes them more fun and colorful for a dessert buffet. Because they have no flour or leavening, they are a great option for Passover sweets. Almond is also a perfect partner for a variety of flavors. The lemon, raspberry, coffee, and chocolate-cherry variations are a tasty and new way to enjoy this classic cookie.

(continued)

If the dough for the amaretti is too sticky, dip your fingers in water as you roll the cookies. This will also help nuts adhere to the top.

Or you can skip the nuts on top and simply roll the cookies in confectioners' sugar before baking.

Bake until golden brown and cool on parchment paper. Don't try to remove the cookies from the parchment paper while they are still warm. After cooling, use a metal spatula to carefully remove the cookies from the parchment paper.

Store each flavor of cookie separately in an airtight container at room temperature. Or freeze in heavy-duty plastic bags for 1 to 2 weeks.

SMALL, SWEET, AND ITALIAN

Lemon-Almond Amaretti*

10 ounces almond paste (or apricot
   kernel paste) broken into pebble-size
   pieces
1/2 cup granulated sugar
1/2 cup confectioners' sugar
1 large egg white
1 teaspoon lemon oil (or extract)
2 teaspoons finely grated lemon zest

A dot of yellow paste food coloring
   (optional)
1 cup sliced almonds (optional)
   or
Confectioners' sugar (optional)

1. Preheat the oven to 350°F. Line baking sheets with parchment paper.
2. In the bowl of a stand mixer fitted with the paddle attachment (or using a hand mixer), combine all of the ingredients except the almonds or confectioners' sugar, if using, and mix on low speed until blended.
3. Increase the speed to medium and mix for 2 minutes to make a sticky dough.
4. Roll the dough into 1-inch balls. Press them into the sliced almonds or roll in confectioners' sugar, if using. Place the cookies on a lined baking sheet, spacing them 2 inches apart. Using your fingers, slightly flatten the tops of the cookies.
5. Bake the cookies for 12 to 15 minutes, or until lightly browned. Remove the baking sheet from the oven. Let the cookies cool on the parchment paper for easiest removal.
6. When the cookies are cool, use a metal spatula to loosen them from the parchment paper.
7. Store in an airtight container.

Makes about 24 cookies

*Wheat-free

Raspberry-Almond Amaretti*

10 ounces almond paste (or apricot kernel paste), broken into pebble-size pieces

1/2 cup granulated sugar

1/2 cup confectioners' sugar

1 extra-large egg white

1 teaspoon raspberry oil (or extract)

A dot of pink paste food coloring (optional)

1 cup sliced almonds (optional)

or

Confectioners' sugar (optional)

1. Preheat the oven to 350°F. Line baking sheets with parchment paper.
2. In the bowl of a stand mixer fitted with the paddle attachment (or using a hand mixer), combine all of the ingredients except the almonds or confectioners' sugar, if using, and mix on low speed until blended.
3. Increase the speed to medium and mix for 2 minutes to make a sticky dough.
4. Roll the dough into 1-inch balls. Press them into the sliced almonds or roll in confectioners' sugar, if using. Place the cookies on lined baking sheets, spacing them 2 inches apart. Using your fingers, slightly flatten the tops of the cookies.
5. Bake the cookies for 12 to 15 minutes, or until lightly browned. Remove the baking sheet from the oven. Let the cookies cool on the parchment paper for easiest removal.
6. When the cookies are cool, use a metal spatula to loosen them from the parchment paper.
7. Store in an airtight container.

Makes about 24 cookies

* Wheat-free

Pies and Tarts

Small pies and tarts always catch my eye when I walk past any pastry shop in Italy. Fruit filled, lattice topped, or simply glazed, they are sure to satisfy any sweet tooth. Pasta Frolla is the traditional Italian pie crust, simply made in a food processor. It can be made 2 to 3 days in advance and kept fresh by wrapping in plastic wrap and refrigerating. Or double wrap the dough and freeze for 1 to 2 weeks.

Many of these pies and tarts have components, especially the Easter Wheat Pies. Read the recipe a few times and try to prep some of the components in advance of assembly. Mangia dolci.

Chocolate-Cherry Amaretti*

10 ounces almond paste (or apricot kernel paste), broken into pebble-size pieces

½ cup granulated sugar

½ cup confectioners' sugar

¼ cup unsweetened Dutch-process cocoa powder

1 teaspoon cherry oil (or extract)

1 extra-large egg white

1 cup sliced almonds

Approximately 24 maraschino cherry halves

1. Preheat the oven to 350°F. Line baking sheets with parchment paper.
2. In the bowl of a stand mixer fitted with the paddle attachment (or using a hand mixer), combine all of the ingredients except the almonds and cherry halves and mix on low speed until blended.
3. Increase the speed to medium and mix for 2 minutes to make a sticky dough.
4. Roll the dough into 1-inch balls. Press them into the sliced almonds. Place the cookies on lined baking sheets, spacing them 2 inches apart. Using your fingers, slightly flatten the tops of the cookies. Press a cherry half into the center of each cookie.
5. Bake the cookies for 12 to 15 minutes, or until lightly browned. Remove the baking sheet from the oven. Let the cookies cool on the parchment paper for easiest removal.
6. When the cookies are cool, use a metal spatula to loosen them from the parchment paper.
7. Store in an airtight container.

Makes about 24 cookies

*Wheat-free

Pistachio Butter Cookies

This is a classic butter cookie with the delicious addition of pistachio paste. Serve them as-is, or half dipped into melted chocolate and sprinkled with finely chopped pistachios.

$1/2$ pound (2 sticks) unsalted butter, softened

$1/2$ cup sugar

$3/4$ cup pistachio paste

1 extra-large egg

$2 1/2$ to $2 3/4$ cups all-purpose flour

$1/2$ teaspoon baking powder

$1/4$ teaspoon salt

Melted chocolate, for dipping (optional)

Chopped pistachios, for sprinkling (optional)

1. Preheat the oven to 350°F. Line baking sheets with parchment paper.
2. In the bowl of a stand mixer fitted with the paddle attachment (or using a hand mixer), cream the butter and sugar on high speed until light. Add the pistachio paste and beat until smooth. Add egg and mix on medium speed until well blended.
3. With the mixer on low speed, gradually add the flour, baking powder, and salt and mix just until blended to form a soft dough.
4. Place the dough into a pastry bag fitted with a star tip. Pipe the dough onto a lined baking sheet, spacing the cookies 2 inches apart.
5. Bake the cookies for 12 to 15 minutes, or until lightly browned. Remove the pan from the oven. Let the cookies cool on the parchment paper.
6. Store at room temperature in an airtight container.

Makes about 40 cookies

OPTIONAL: Dip half of each cookie into melted chocolate and sprinkle with chopped pistachios. Let dry on parchment paper.

Espresso Meringues*

Meringues are one of my favorite sweets to keep in the house. I'll bake a batch, then enjoy one each evening with an after-dinner espresso. These miniature meringues fit perfectly, served on a saucer. One day I was baking and was out of extracts. I found a bottle of anisette that had a coffee flavor as well, and added 2 tablespoons to flavor my meringues. Instant favorite!

4 extra-large egg whites

1 cup sugar

2 tablespoons coffee/anisette liqueur

1. Preheat the oven to 225°F. Line baking sheets with parchment paper.
2. In the bowl of a stand mixer fitted with the wire whisk attachment (or using a hand mixer), beat the egg whites on high speed until soft peaks form. Gradually add the sugar and coffee flavoring and beat until stiff peaks form.
3. Fill a pastry bag with the egg white mixture. Cut off the tip of the pastry bag to make a small opening. Pipe the mixture into 1-inch rounds on the lined baking sheet.
4. Bake the meringues for 1½ hours, or until dry. Turn the oven off. Leave the meringues in the oven overnight.

Makes 60 meringues

*Wheat-free

Apricot-Walnut Biscottini

Authentic biscotti like these do not use any fat, such as butter. They are less "cookielike" and are perfect for dunking. They have a great shelf life, so my cookie jar at home is always fully stocked.

1½ cups all-purpose flour, plus additional ¼ cup, if needed

1 cup sugar

2 teaspoons baking powder

¼ teaspoon salt

1 teaspoon ground cinnamon

1 cup dried apricots, coarsely chopped

1 cup walnuts, coarsely chopped

3 extra-large eggs

2 teaspoons pure vanilla extract

1 large egg, lightly beaten

1. Preheat the oven to 350°F. Line baking sheets with parchment paper.
2. In a large mixing bowl, combine the flour, sugar, baking powder, salt, cinnamon, apricots, and walnuts and mix until blended.
3. In a small mixing bowl, whisk the eggs and vanilla. Add the egg mixture to the flour mixture and mix until blended; the dough should be soft, but not sticky. If the dough is sticky, knead in an additional ¼ cup flour.
4. Turn the dough out onto a lightly floured surface. Divide the dough into 3 equal pieces.
5. Roll each piece of dough into a loaf about 10 inches long. Place them on a lined baking sheet, spacing them 4 inches apart. Gently press to flatten the tops slightly.
6. Using a pastry brush, brush the tops of the loaves with beaten egg.
7. Bake the loaves for 15 to 20 minutes, or until golden brown.

8. Remove the baking sheet from the oven. Cool the loaves on the baking sheet.

9. Place the cooled loaves on a cutting board. Carefully, slice them diagonally into ½-inch-wide slices.

10. Place the biscottini in a single layer on the baking sheet and return to the oven. Bake for 8 to 10 minutes, or until lightly toasted. Remove the pan from the oven. Transfer the biscottini to wire racks to cool.

11. Store the biscottini in airtight container.

Makes 36 biscottini

BISCOTTI BASICS

Biscotti in Italian literally means "twice-baked." The cookies are first molded into a cylinder and baked, then cooled, sliced, and toasted again.

Biscottini are small biscotti, usually 2 or 3 bites; "-ini" means "tiny."

Traditional Italian biscotti like the Apricot-Walnut Biscottini have no butter or shortening. This will make them hard and crispy and perfect for dunking into coffee or a glass of Vin Santo. Full of nuts, dried fruit, and spices, biscotti is actually a healthy cookie option. All regions of Italy have various flavors of biscotti based on locally grown nuts and fruit.

Legend has it that Columbus packed biscotti for his historic trip because of the long shelf life.

Some of our other biscotti flavors are butter-based and use the creaming method. This makes them more "cookielike" and more suited to the American palate.

BISCOTTI-MAKING TIPS

- If your dough is sticky, dust it with additional flour to make it easier to form into loaves.
- Be sure to bake the biscotti on parchment paper.
- Cool before slicing.
- Slice the biscotti diagonally into $1/2$-inch slices and return to the baking sheet in a single layer for toasting.

Store biscotti at room temperature in an airtight container.

Mocha Chip Biscottini

Chocolate and a rich coffee flavor make these much-loved biscottini. Egg wash and a sprinkle of coarse sugar before baking gives them a special sparkle, perfect for a holiday cookie tray.

2 tablespoons instant espresso

1 tablespoon hot water

1/2 pound (2 sticks) unsalted butter, softened

1 cup sugar

5 extra-large eggs

4 cups all-purpose flour

1/2 teaspoon baking powder

1/4 teaspoon salt

2 cups chocolate chips

Coarse sugar, or additional sugar, for sprinkling

1. Preheat the oven to 350°F. Line baking sheets with parchment paper.

2. In a small bowl, dissolve the instant espresso in the hot water. Set aside.

3. In the bowl of a stand mixer fitted with the paddle attachment (or using a hand mixer), cream the butter and sugar on medium-high speed until light. Add 4 of the eggs and the espresso mixture and mix well on medium speed.

4. With the mixer on low speed, gradually add the flour, baking powder, and salt and mix just until incorporated. Stir in the chocolate chips.

5. Turn the dough out onto a lightly floured surface. Divide the dough into 6 equal pieces. Roll each piece into a loaf 10 to 12 inches long. Place the loaves on the lined baking sheets, spacing them 3 inches apart. Gently press to flatten the tops slightly.

6. In a small bowl, beat the remaining 1 egg. Using a pastry brush, brush the tops of the loaves with the beaten egg and sprinkle with coarse sugar.

7. Bake the loaves for 15 to 20 minutes, until golden brown.

8. Remove the baking sheets from the oven. Cool the loaves on the baking sheets or transfer to a wire rack to cool.

9. Place the cooled loaves on a cutting board. Carefully slice the loaves, diagonally, into ½-inch-wide slices.

10. Return the slices to the baking sheets in a single layer. Bake the biscottini for another 8 to 12 minutes, or until lightly toasted. Remove the baking sheets from the oven.

11. Transfer the biscottini to wire rack to cool. Store in an airtight container.

Makes about 60 biscottini

Raspberry Biscottini with Chocolate Drizzle

These tasty sweets are one of our most popular flavors of biscottini.
The cakelike raspberry texture is perfectly paired with a hefty drizzle of
melted chocolate.

8 tablespoons (1 stick) unsalted butter,
   softened
$1/2$ cup sugar
2 extra-large eggs
$1/2$ teaspoon raspberry oil (or extract)
$1/4$ cup raspberry pie filling

3 cups all-purpose flour
$1/4$ teaspoon baking powder
Pinch of salt
$1/2$ cup chocolate chips

1. Preheat the oven to 350°F. Line baking sheets with parchment paper.
2. In the bowl of a stand mixer fitted with the paddle attachment (or using a hand mixer), cream the butter and sugar on medium-high speed until light. Add the eggs, raspberry oil, and raspberry filling and mix well.
3. With the mixer on low speed, gradually add the flour, baking powder, and salt and mix just until incorporated.
4. Turn the dough out onto a lightly floured surface. Divide the dough into 3 equal pieces. Roll each piece into a loaf 10 to 12 inches long. Place the loaves on the lined baking sheet, spacing them 3 inches apart. Gently press to flatten the tops slightly.
5. Bake the loaves for 15 to 20 minutes, until golden brown.
6. Remove the baking sheet from the oven. Cool the loaves on the baking sheet or transfer to a wire rack to cool.

7. Place the cooled loaves on a cutting board. Carefully slice the loaves, diagonally, into ½-inch-wide slices.

8. Return the slices to the baking sheet in a single layer. Bake the biscottini for another 8 to 12 minutes, or until lightly toasted. Remove the baking sheet from the oven.

9. Cool the biscottini on the baking sheet. Stack the biscottini upright for the drizzle.

10. In a double boiler or in a stainless-steel bowl set over a saucepan of simmering water, or in the microwave, melt the chocolate. Using a fork, drizzle the melted chocolate over the tops of the biscottini.

11. Store in an airtight container.

Makes about 36 biscottini

Pumpkin Biscottini

BISCOTTINI DI ZUCCA

A seasonal favorite, these biscottini are almost savory, perfect with a hearty autumn zuppa. *With cinnamon icing, they sweeten up any day.*

Biscottini

$^3/_4$ pound (3 sticks) unsalted butter, softened

1 cup granulated sugar

$^1/_2$ cup brown sugar

3 extra-large eggs

1 cup canned pure pumpkin purée

4 cups all-purpose flour, plus more as needed

3 teaspoons ground cinnamon

1$^1/_2$ teaspoons baking powder

$^1/_2$ teaspoon ground cloves

$^1/_2$ teaspoon freshly grated nutmeg

$^1/_2$ teaspoon salt

Cinnamon Icing

2 cups confectioners' sugar

2 to 3 tablespoons water

1 teaspoon ground cinnamon

MAKE THE BISCOTTINI

1. Preheat the oven to 350°F. Line baking sheets with parchment paper.
2. In the bowl of a stand mixer fitted with the paddle attachment (or using a hand mixer), cream the butter and the granulated and brown sugars on medium-high speed until light. Add the eggs and pumpkin purée and mix well on medium speed.
3. With the mixer on low speed, add the flour, cinnamon, baking powder, cloves, nutmeg, and salt and mix until well blended.

4. Turn the dough out onto a lightly floured surface; the dough should be soft but not sticky. If sticky, knead in additional flour. Divide the dough into 5 equal pieces. Roll each piece into a loaf about 12 inches long. Place the loaves on the lined baking sheets, spacing them 4 inches apart.

5. Bake the loaves for 20 to 25 minutes, or until golden brown. Cool the loaves on the baking sheets or transfer to a wire rack to cool.

6. Place the cooled loaves on a cutting board. Carefully slice the loaves, diagonally, into ½-inch-wide slices.

7. Return the cookies to the baking sheets in a single layer. Bake the biscottini for another 10 to 15 minutes, or until lightly browned.

8. Remove the baking sheets from the oven. Cool the biscottini on the baking sheet. Stack the biscottini upright for the drizzle.

MAKE THE ICING

9. Combine the confectioners' sugar, water, and cinnamon and mix until smooth. Using a fork, generously drizzle the icing over the tops of the biscottini. Let dry for 1 to 2 hours, or overnight.

Makes about 48 biscottini

Double Chocolate–Almond Biscottini

Chocolate chips and almonds give this decadent biscottini tons of flavor. Be sure to use Dutch-process cocoa for the fullest flavor.

½ pound (2 sticks) unsalted butter

1 cup sugar

4 extra-large eggs

2½ cups all-purpose flour

1 cup unsweetened Dutch-process cocoa
    powder

½ teaspoon baking powder

¼ teaspoon salt

1 cup semisweet chocolate chips

1 cup almonds, coarsely chopped

1. Preheat the oven to 350°F. Line baking sheets with parchment paper.
2. In the bowl of a stand mixer fitted with the paddle attachment (or using a hand mixer), cream the butter and sugar on medium-high speed until light. Add the eggs and mix until well blended.
3. With the mixer on low speed, gradually add the flour, cocoa, baking powder, and salt and mix just until incorporated. Stir in the chocolate chips and almonds.
4. Turn the dough out onto a lightly floured surface. Divide the dough into 6 equal pieces. Roll each piece into a loaf 10 to 12 inches long. Place the loaves on the lined baking sheets, spacing them 3 inches apart. Gently press to flatten the tops slightly.
5. Bake the loaves for 15 to 20 minutes, until firm.
6. Remove the baking sheets from the oven. Cool the loaves on the baking sheets or transfer to a wire rack to cool.

7. Place the cooled loaves on a cutting board. Carefully slice the loaves, diagonally, into ½-inch-wide slices.

8. Return the slices to the baking sheets in a single layer. Bake the biscottini for another 8 to 12 minutes, or until lightly toasted.

9. Remove the baking sheets from the oven. Cool the biscottini on the baking sheets.

Makes about 50 biscottini

Nutella Thumbprints

A classic cookie redefined, Italian-style! A simple squirt of Nutella in the center makes these a rich and gooey new favorite. Be sure to fill these thumbprints after they are baked and cooled.

1/2 pound (2 sticks) unsalted butter, softened

1/2 cup sugar

2 extra-large egg yolks

1 teaspoon pure vanilla extract

2 1/2 cups all-purpose flour

1/4 teaspoon salt

1 cup hazelnut spread (such as Nutella)

1. Preheat the oven to 350°F. Line baking sheets with parchment paper.
2. In the bowl of a stand mixer fitted with the paddle attachment (or using a hand mixer), cream the butter and sugar on medium-high speed until light. Add the egg yolks and vanilla and mix on medium speed until well blended.
3. With the mixer on low speed, gradually add the flour and salt and mix just until blended.
4. Roll the dough into 1/2-inch balls. Place the balls on the lined baking sheets, spacing them 2 inches apart. Press the tops slightly to flatten. Using your fingertip, indent the center of each cookie to make a well.
5. Bake the cookies for 10 to 15 minutes, or until lightly browned. After 5 minutes in the oven, check the cookies. Keep pressing the wells in the centers of the cookies with the back of a small spoon. Press every 5 minutes until the cookies are done, just to be sure the wells are intact.

6. Remove the baking sheets from the oven. Cool the cookies on the parchment paper or transfer to a wire rack to cool. Cool the cookies completely before filling.

7. Using a pastry bag or spoon, fill the centers of the cookies with the Nutella.

Makes about 36 cookies

Sicilian Fig Cookies

CUCCIDATI

This fig-and-nut-filled cookie is a Sicilian tradition. I love the simple presentation of a light egg wash and a sprinkling of coarse sugar before baking. Or you can dress them up for the holidays with a drizzle of icing and sprinkles after baking and cooling. Baker's choice—either way, delicioso!

Cookies

2 1/2 cups all-purpose flour

1/2 cup granulated sugar

1 teaspoon baking powder

1/4 teaspoon salt

4 tablespoons (1/2 stick) unsalted butter

2 extra-large eggs

1/4 cup whole milk

2 tablespoons whiskey

2 tablespoons orange marmalade

1 teaspoon ground cinnamon

1 egg, lightly beaten (egg wash)
   (optional)

Coarse sugar (optional)

Filling

8 ounces dried figs

1/2 cup large walnut pieces

2 tablespoons granulated sugar

Icing (optional)

1 cup 6-X confectioners' sugar

2 tablespoons water

1 tablespoon whiskey

MAKE THE COOKIE DOUGH

1. In a food processor, combine the flour, granulated sugar, baking powder, and salt and pulse until blended. Add the butter and pulse until the mixture is uniform. Add the eggs and milk and pulse to make a smooth dough.

2. Turn the dough out onto a lightly floured surface. Knead to make a smooth, soft dough. Wrap in plastic wrap and refrigerate overnight.

MAKE THE FILLING

3. In a food processor, combine all of the ingredients and pulse until blended and slightly chunky. Set aside.

ASSEMBLE THE COOKIES

4. Preheat the oven to 350°F. Line baking sheets with parchment paper.
5. Divide the dough into 4 equal pieces. Refrigerate 3 pieces of the dough. Roll 1 piece out on a lightly floured surface into a rectangle ⅛ inch thick and approximately 13 inches long and 6 inches wide. Place one-quarter of the filling in the middle of the dough. Fold the dough over the filling jelly-roll-style and press to seal. Making sure the seam is on the bottom, brush with the beaten egg and sprinkle with coarse sugar. (Or omit the egg wash and sugar and leave plain. Ice when cooled.) Cut the roll into ½-inch slices. Place them on the lined baking sheets, seam sides down, spacing them 2 inches apart.
6. Bake the cookies for 15 to 20 minutes, or until golden brown.
7. Remove the baking sheets from the oven. Cool the cookies on the parchment paper. If not egg washed and sugared, cool the cookies completely and then ice with confectioners' sugar icing.

MAKE THE ICING (OPTIONAL)

8. In a small bowl, combine all of the ingredients and stir until smooth. Drizzle over the cooled cookies, if desired.

Makes about 50 cookies

Cinnamon-Walnut Florentines

Light, crispy, and supersweet (in a good way!), these lacy crispy cookies are ideal filled with chocolate as sandwich cookies, or simply crumbled over gelato.

1/4 cup all-purpose flour

1 1/2 cups walnuts, finely chopped

1/4 teaspoon ground cinnamon

4 tablespoons (1/2 stick) unsalted butter

2 tablespoons heavy cream

2 tablespoons honey

3/4 cup sugar

1. Preheat the oven to 350°F. Line baking sheets with parchment paper.
2. In a small bowl, combine the flour, walnuts, and cinnamon. Set aside.
3. In a small saucepan, heat the butter, heavy cream, honey, and sugar over medium heat. Bring to a boil, stirring constantly. Remove from the heat and stir in the walnut mixture.
4. Spoon the dough with a small spoon (demitasse) onto the lined baking sheets, spacing the cookies 4 inches apart. Flatten the tops of the cookies.
5. Bake the cookies for 10 to 15 minutes, or until uniformly golden brown.
6. Remove the baking sheets from the oven. Cool the cookies on the parchment paper.

Makes about 36 cookies

Polenta Cookies

Chewy yet slightly crispy, be careful not to overbake these cookies. The cornmeal adds a rustic texture to the lightly sweetened cookies. Enjoy them plain or sandwiched with orange or apricot preserves.

1³/₄ cups all-purpose flour

1¹/₄ cups cornmeal

1 teaspoon baking soda

¹/₂ teaspoon salt

¹/₂ pound (2 sticks) unsalted butter, softened

1¹/₂ cups sugar

2 extra-large eggs

1 teaspoon pure vanilla extract

1. Preheat the oven to 350°F. Line baking sheets with parchment paper.
2. In a small bowl, combine the flour, cornmeal, baking soda, and salt.
3. In the bowl of a stand mixer fitted with the paddle attachment (or using a hand mixer), cream the butter and sugar on medium-high speed until light. Add the eggs and vanilla and mix on medium speed until blended.
4. With the mixer on low speed, add flour mixture and mix just until blended.
5. Roll the dough into ½-inch balls and place them on the lined baking sheets, spacing them 2 inches apart.
6. Bake the cookies for 10 to 12 minutes, or until the edges begin to brown.
7. Remove the baking sheets from the oven. Transfer the cookies to wire racks to cool.

Makes about 50 cookies

Susan's Taralles

Many paese in Italy have a version of these simple twisted cookies. They are usually flavored differently in each town. My friend Susan's family bakes these cookies with a combination of three extracts: vanilla, lemon, and anise. They give an otherwise plain biscuit a mysterious herbal flavor. A simple lemon icing sweetens them deliciously.

Cookies

3 extra-large eggs

$1/2$ cup granulated sugar

$1/4$ cup vegetable oil

$1/2$ teaspoon lemon extract

$1/2$ teaspoon pure vanilla extract

$1/2$ teaspoon anise extract

$2^1/2$ to 3 cups all-purpose flour

Pinch of salt

1 teaspoon baking powder

Lemon Icing

3 cups confectioners' sugar

1 teaspoon lemon extract

$1/4$ cup water

1 teaspoon finely grated lemon zest (optional)

MAKE THE COOKIES

1. Preheat the oven to 350°F. Line baking sheets with parchment paper.
2. In the bowl of a stand mixer fitted with the paddle attachment (or using a hand mixer), combine the eggs, sugar, oil, and extracts, and beat on medium speed until blended.
3. With the mixer on low speed, add 2 cups of flour, the salt, and the baking powder, and mix until blended.

4. Turn the dough out onto a floured surface. Knead in additional flour as needed to make a soft, but not sticky, dough. Roll the dough into pencil-thick pieces about 4 inches long. Twist them into knots or wrap into rounds. Place them on the lined baking sheets, spacing them 2 inches apart.

5. Bake the cookies for 12 to 15 minutes, or until the edges are lightly browned.

6. Remove the baking sheets from the oven. Cool the cookies on the sheets. Cool completely before icing.

MAKE THE ICING

7. In the bowl of a stand mixer fitted with the paddle attachment (or using a hand mixer), combine all of the ingredients except the lemon zest, if using, and mix until smooth.

8. Using a metal spatula, frost the tops of the cookies; the icing will run down the sides. Sprinkle the wet icing with the lemon zest, if desired.

9. Let the icing dry before stacking or serving.

Makes 40 to 50 cookies

Brown Sugar Pizzelles

These mini pizzelles are simply made by dropping a small amount of dough onto a classic pizzelle iron. They are perfect on their own or stacked three high, layered with whipped cream and fresh fruit.

2 cups all-purpose flour

2 teaspoons baking powder

1/2 teaspoon ground cinnamon

3 extra-large eggs

1 cup lightly packed brown sugar

8 tablespoons (1 stick) unsalted butter, melted and cooled

Confectioners' sugar, for dusting

  or

Whipped cream and fruit

1. Preheat a pizzelle iron according to the manufacturer's directions.
2. In a small bowl, combine the flour, baking powder, and cinnamon.
3. In the bowl of a stand mixer fitted with the paddle attachment (or using a hand mixer), beat the eggs and brown sugar on medium speed. Add the melted butter and mix until blended.
4. With the mixer on low speed, gradually add the flour mixture and mix to make a sticky dough.
5. Drop half a teaspoon of dough onto the hot iron, close, and bake until golden brown, 40 to 50 seconds.
6. Serve lightly dusted with confectioners' sugar, or layer and stack with whipped cream and fruit.

Makes about 55 mini pizzelles

Puddings and Custards

Puddings and custards are great make-ahead desserts that are always crowd-pleasers. Classic Italian flavors like Arborio rice pudding and chocolate-espresso pudding with sambuca cream are updated just by presentation: shot glasses or vintage Champagne glasses. Bellissimo!

Buttermilk Panna Cotta with Crushed Amaretti and Berries

Chocolate-Espresso Pudding with Sambuca Cream (*Budino di Cioccolato*)

Arborio Rice Pudding Parfaits with Plum and Barolo Sauce

Tiramisu Bread Pudding (*Dolce di Pane*)

Buttermilk Panna Cotta with Crushed Amaretti and Berries*

In Italian, panna cotta means "cooked cream." This smooth and creamy panna cotta is a tasty variation on the classic. A tiny touch of sour from the buttermilk makes this dessert a make-ahead family favorite.

1 cup buttermilk

4 teaspoons unflavored gelatin

2 1/2 cups heavy cream

1/2 cup sugar

2 tablespoons amaretto

2 cups mixed fresh berries

1 cup crushed amaretti cookies

   (see page xxi)

1. Spray six 1/2-cup ramekins with nonstick cooking spray. Set aside.
2. Pour 1/2 cup of the buttermilk into a small bowl. Sprinkle with the gelatin and let stand for 10 minutes to soften.
3. In a medium saucepan, combine the remaining 1/2 cup buttermilk, the cream, and the sugar and whisk over medium heat until boiling. Remove from the heat, stir in the gelatin mixture, and whisk until dissolved. Stir in the amaretto.
4. Pour the mixture into the prepared ramekins, cover with plastic wrap, and refrigerate overnight. Serve in the ramekins, or to remove the panna cottas, loosen the edges with a knife and turn the ramekins upside down on individual dessert plates.
5. Top the panna cotta with fresh berries and crushed amaretti.

Makes six 1/2-cup panna cottas

*Wheat-free

Chocolate-Espresso Pudding with Sambuca Cream*

BUDINO DI CIOCCOLATO

This rich chocolate and coffee pudding is perfect topped with a dollop of sambuca cream. For maximum flavor and convenience, make these puddings a day in advance. Refrigerate them right in the serving glasses and top with cream just before serving. Add a biscottini for a complete Italian treat.

Pudding

2 cups whole milk

1/2 cup sugar

1/2 cup unsweetened Dutch-process
    cocoa powder

1 teaspoon instant espresso

3 extra-large egg yolks

4 teaspoons cornstarch

1/2 cup semisweet chocolate chips

Sambuca Cream

1/2 cup heavy cream

1/4 cup sugar

1/4 cup sambuca

MAKE THE PUDDING

1. In a medium saucepan over medium-high heat, combine 1½ cups of the milk, the sugar, cocoa, and espresso and whisk until simmering.

2. In a medium bowl, whisk the egg yolks, cornstarch, and the remaining ½ cup milk. Gradually add the warm milk mixture into the egg mixture, in a thin stream.

3. Return the mixture to the saucepan and heat over low heat, whisking constantly until mixture is boiling and thick.

4. Remove the pan from the heat, add the chocolate chips, and stir until the chocolate has melted and is smooth.

5. Pour the pudding into 2-ounce shot glasses or small cups. Cover the tops of the puddings directly with plastic wrap to prevent a skin from forming. Refrigerate overnight.

MAKE THE SAMBUCA CREAM

6. In the bowl of a stand mixer fitted with the wire whisk attachment (or using a hand mixer), whip the cream on high speed until soft peaks form. Add the sugar and sambuca and continue to whip until stiff.

7. Fill a pastry bag with the cream. Cut off the tip of the pastry bag to make a small opening. Squeeze the bag to release the cream and pipe a swirl on top of each pudding.

Makes six ½-cup puddings

*Wheat-free

Arborio Rice Pudding Parfaits with Plum and Barolo Sauce*

Creamy rice pudding gets paired with a tasty sauce of plum and red wine in this updated dessert. Layer the rice pudding and sauce for full visual impact. Another easy one and sure to impress.

Plum and Barolo Sauce

1 cup dried plums, chopped

2 tablespoons sugar

1 cup Barolo, or other full-bodied
    red wine

Rice Pudding

$1/2$ cup Arborio rice

$1/4$ cup heavy cream

$1^1/2$ cups whole milk

$1/4$ cup sugar

MAKE THE SAUCE

1. In a small saucepan, combine the plums, sugar, and wine. Bring to a boil over medium heat. Reduce the heat to low and simmer, uncovered, for 20 to 25 minutes.

2. Remove from the heat. Set aside.

MAKE THE RICE PUDDING

3. In a small saucepan, combine the rice, heavy cream, milk, and sugar and bring to a boil over medium heat. Reduce the heat to low and simmer, stirring occasionally, for 25 to 30 minutes, or until the rice is al dente. Remove from the heat. Cool slightly.

4. Drop a heaping tablespoon of rice pudding into the bottom of each of eight 2-ounce shot glasses. Top each with a spoonful of the plum sauce. Continue layering the pudding and plum sauce in each shot glass.

5. Cover the tops of the glasses with plastic wrap and refrigerate overnight.
6. Serve chilled.

Makes 8 pudding parfaits

*Wheat-free

Tiramisu Bread Puddings

DOLCE DI PANE

Italians love to recycle, so why not use leftover bread to bake this delicious treat? Simply soak the bread in fresh-brewed espresso and layer with sweetened mascarpone for a warm, comforting dessert.

$^{1}/_{2}$ cup espresso

6 cups cubed challah bread

3 extra-large eggs

1 cup sugar

2 cups mascarpone cheese

Ice cream or sweetened whipped cream, for serving

1. Preheat the oven to 350°F. Butter six $^{1}/_{2}$-cup ramekins. Set aside.
2. In a small bowl, pour the espresso over the cubed bread and toss to coat the bread. Set aside.
3. In a medium bowl, beat the eggs. Whisk in the sugar and mascarpone and continue to whisk until smooth.
4. Stir in the soaked bread, cover, and refrigerate for 15 to 20 minutes.
5. Ladle the mixture into the prepared ramekins. Place the ramekins on a sturdy baking sheet. Bake the puddings for 25 to 30 minutes, or until the centers are puffed and a cake tester inserted into the middle comes out clean.
6. Serve warm with ice cream or sweetened whipped cream.

Makes six $^{1}/_{2}$-cup puddings

Frozen Desserts

Sometimes something cold is the perfect ending to a great Italian meal. Gelato, semi-freddos, and granitas are perfect for any season or occasion. Frozen desserts are always great to keep premade in the freezer for unexpected guests or midnight cravings. Magnifico!

Mini Raspberry-Hazelnut Zucotto

Ice Cream Truffles *(Tartufi)*

    Chocolate Coffee Tartufo

    White Chocolate–Pistachio Tartufo

Strawberry-Prosecco Granita

Cherry-Vanilla Semifreddo with
    Chocolate Sauce

Affogato

Chocolate-Almond Biscotti Ice-Cream
    Sandwiches

Mini Raspberry-Hazelnut Zucotto

With origins in Florence, these funky little duomos, *or domes, are a colorful and unique dessert to serve. The color comes from the hot pink of the raspberries and the ice cream. You'll need tiny round half-sphere molds for these, or you can substitute ramekins. Just be sure to work quickly so the ice cream stays a bit firm during assembly.*

30 ladyfinger cookies (approximately)

1 pint raspberry ice cream or gelato

1 cup raspberries, fresh or frozen

$1/2$ cup chopped hazelnuts

1. Line 3-inch/$1/2$-cup molds with plastic wrap. Let the wrap hang over the edges of the mold.
2. Press 3 ladyfingers into a half-sphere mold. Add 1 scoop of ice cream. Top with 1 tablespoon of the raspberries and press firmly into mold. Top with a bit more ice cream, then the hazelnuts and pack firmly into the mold, working somewhat quickly so that the ice cream doesn't melt.
3. Top with more ladyfingers. Press firmly, then cover the bottom of the zucotto with the overhanging plastic wrap. Repeat to fill all the molds.
4. Place the filled molds in the freezer and freeze for 2 or 3 hours, or overnight. (The molds can be kept in the freezer for 1 to 2 weeks.)
5. To serve, remove the molds from the freezer. Unwrap the plastic wrap and invert the molds onto individual dessert plates to release the zucotto. Remove the plastic wrap. Place in paper liners, if desired, and serve.

Makes about 6 zucotto

Ice Cream Truffles

TARTUFI!

Named for their savory counterpart, these tartufi, or mushroom-shaped ice-cream balls, are a refreshing sweet treat. It only took one visit to the birthplace of tartufo, the Roman ristorante Tre Scalini, and I was hooked. Their classic version is made with vanilla gelato with a cherry in the center, rolled in chocolate pieces, and topped with whipped cream. It's a must-taste for any trip to Rome, and a great inspiration. They've been making tartufi since 1946.

Use these recipes as a guideline, but feel free to create your own favorite frozen flavor combination. The sky's the limit! Choose your favorite ice cream and roll it in an assortment of coconut, nuts, cookie crumbs, and more. These are perfect for making ahead and storing in the freezer for those unexpected times an amazing dessert needs to happen.

TARTUFI-MAKING TIPS

- Thaw the ice cream slightly so you can fill and mold it into a ball.
- Work quickly so that the ice cream doesn't melt.
- You can use a cake pop pan to mold the ice cream into a perfect sphere, but an ice cream scoop will work the same.

- Be sure to add a surprise in the center—a piece of chocolate or white chocolate and a maraschino cherry are just a few ideas.
- Get your outer coverings—biscotti crumbs, sprinkles, etc.—ready and place them on a flat plate. This will make it easier for you to coat the ice cream balls.
- Keep the tartufi frozen until serving time.
- Serve an assortment of flavors with your favorite ice cream sauce.

CHOCOLATE COFFEE TARTUFO

1 pint coffee ice cream, slightly softened

10 chocolate-covered espresso beans

1½ cups semisweet chocolate chips, finely chopped

1. Scoop the ice cream into 10 portions. Use the ice-cream scoop to help form each portion into a ball. Push 1 chocolate-covered coffee bean into the center of each ice cream ball.
2. Roll the balls in the chopped chocolate.
3. Place the tartufi on parchment paper–lined baking sheets and place them in the freezer until serving time.
4. Serve the tartufi in paper liners, if desired.

Makes 10 tartufi

WHITE CHOCOLATE-PISTACHIO TARTUFO

1 pint vanilla ice cream, slightly softened

10 pieces white chocolate

2 cups pistachios, finely chopped

1. Scoop the ice cream into 10 portions. Use the ice-cream scoop to help form each portion into a ball. Push 1 piece of white chocolate into the center of each ice cream ball.
2. Roll the balls in the chopped pistachios.
3. Place the tartufi on parchment paper–lined baking sheets and place them in the freezer until serving time.
4. Serve the tartufi in paper liners, if desired.

Makes 10 tartufi

OTHER GREAT TARTUFI IDEAS

- Be creative, think sprinkles!
- Vanilla ice cream, caramel candy center, toasted coconut coating
- Strawberry ice cream, chocolate center, chocolate coating
- Vanilla ice cream, peanut butter center, graham cracker coating
- Vanilla ice cream, almond center, crushed amaretti coating
- Chocolate ice cream, raspberry center, crushed cookie crumb coating

Strawberry-Prosecco Granita*

This delicious shaved ice is a great summer refresher. For maximum flavor, be sure to use strawberries at their peak of ripeness. Serve in tall shot glasses or vintage wineglasses.

1 cup water
1/2 cup sugar

1 cup puréed strawberries
1/4 cup prosecco

1. In a small saucepan over medium heat, combine the water and sugar, and bring to a boil, stirring. Let boil for 2 or 3 minutes, or until the sugar has dissolved. Remove from the heat.
2. Stir in the strawberries and prosecco.
3. Pour the mixture into a shallow, nonreactive baking pan or bowl. Place the pan in the freezer for 2 to 3 hours.
4. Remove from the freezer. Using a fork, shave the ice into flakes. Spoon the shaved ice into shot glasses or shallow wineglasses. Freeze until ready to serve.

Makes four 1/2-cup servings
*Wheat-free

Cherry-Vanilla Semifreddo with Chocolate Sauce*

This creamy treat is ideal drizzled with a rich chocolate sauce. You can simply spoon the mixture into a plastic wrap–lined loaf pan, and scoop as ice cream when needed, or freeze in individual round pans or loaf pans. Served with a biscottini, this is the perfect make-ahead dessert.

Semifreddo

3 extra-large eggs

$3/4$ cup sugar

1 teaspoon pure vanilla extract

$1^1/2$ cups heavy cream

$1^1/2$ cups cherries, pitted and coarsely chopped

Chocolate Sauce

1 cup heavy cream

$1/2$ cup corn syrup

8 ounces semisweet chocolate, finely chopped

MAKE THE SEMIFREDDO

1. Line six $1/2$-cup ramekins with plastic wrap. (Or line a full-size loaf pan.) Let excess plastic wrap hang over the sides. Set aside.

2. In a double boiler, or in a stainless-steel bowl set over a saucepan of simmering water, whip the eggs and sugar with a hand mixer until thick and very light in color. Add the vanilla.

3. Remove the egg mixture from the heat and let cool.

4. In the bowl of a stand mixer fitted with the wire whisk attachment, whip the cream on high speed until stiff.

5. Gently fold the whipped cream into the cooled egg mixture. Fold in the cherries.

6. Pour the mixture into the prepared ramekins or pan, filling them to the top. Cover the semifreddo with the excess, overhanging plastic wrap.

7. Place in freezer overnight.

MAKE THE SAUCE

8. In a small saucepan over low heat, combine the cream and corn syrup and bring to a boil. Pour the mixture over the chocolate in a bowl. Stir to melt the chocolate. Use immediately. (The sauce can be made 2 to 3 days in advance. Store, refrigerated, in an airtight container. Gently rewarm before using.)

9. To serve, gently tug on the plastic wrap to help remove the semifreddo from the ramekins. (Or scoop from the full-size loaf pan into bowls.) Remove and discard the plastic wrap. Drizzle the semifreddo with chocolate sauce.

10. Serve immediately.

Makes 6 servings semifreddo
*Wheat-free

Affogato*

The simplest Italian dessert by far! From the Italian word for "drowned," affogato offers a quick fix when you need sugar, caffeine, and a little something stronger. Simply drown gelato with espresso and vermouth for an icy espresso martini.

Vanilla gelato, 1 scoop per person
Vermouth, 1 shot per person
Espresso, 1 shot per person

1. Place 1 scoop of ice cream into a small bowl. Repeat for as many servings as needed. Pour 1 shot of vermouth over the ice cream, then a shot of espresso.
2. Grab a spoon and enjoy!

*Wheat-free

Chocolate-Almond Biscotti Ice-Cream Sandwiches

Why not try this Italian version of a classic American tradition? Two chocolate-almond biscotti are sandwiched with the ice cream of your choice—chocolate, vanilla, strawberry, and more. Tutti bene.

1 pint ice cream of your choice
30 chocolate-almond biscotti, sliced thin
  (about ¼ inch thick)

1. Slightly soften the ice cream.
2. Spread about 2 tablespoons of the ice cream in a thin layer on a biscotti. Top with another biscotti. Repeat with the remaining ice cream and biscotti.
3. Freeze until serving time.

Makes 15 ice-cream sandwiches

One Last Tiny Treat

Stuffed Dates*

These tasty treats are one of my mother-in-law's specialties. She still makes them every Christmas for her sweets buffet to keep the tradition, and I eat them and take a few home to be sure she keeps making them. They can satisfy your sweet tooth in any season, and are good for you. I mean, fruit and roasted nuts, right?

Approximately 20 whole almonds, roasted
One 8-ounce container whole dates, pitted
Granulated sugar, for rolling

1. Preheat the oven to 400°F. Line a baking sheet with parchment paper.
2. Spread out the almonds on the lined baking sheet.
3. Bake the almonds for 15 to 20 minutes, or until nicely toasted. Remove from the oven. Set aside to cool.
4. Using a paring knife, make a slit in the top of each date. Stuff each date with 1 or 2 almonds. Roll the dates in sugar to coat. Place in paper liners.
5. Serve at room temperature. (The dates can be made 4 or 5 days in advance. Store, refrigerated, in an airtight container. Re-sugar as needed.)

*Wheat-free

Sources

EQUIPMENT

Nordicware manufactures some of the finest small tart and pie pans in cast iron and with non-stick surfaces. Plus, they are made in the United States. Order online at www.nordicware .com or find them in most kitchen shops. Some items are available at Target and Walmart.

For small stoneware pie dishes, I love Le Creuset (www.lecreuset.com). Their pretty and colorful petite tart pans are a nice way to serve mini pies. No de-panning necessary!

Pamperedchef.com also offers great utensils and bakeware.

CUPCAKE LINERS

Most times I use standard cupcake liners. Use your local party store as a resource for mini, standard, and jumbo liners.

Check www.wilton.com for an assortment of patterns. Wilton also has everything you'll need for baking and candy making.

There are many fun ideas at www.shopsweetlulu.com.

INGREDIENTS

Nuts.com has an amazing assortment of nuts, dried fruit, and more, plus they have a great sense of humor. One order and you'll see why.

American Almond (www.americanalmond.com) is a professional baker's dream come true. Their products and service are unmatched. They are an excellent source for almond, kernel, and pistachio pastes. They have a great Web site (www.lovenbake.com) with recipes for the home baker as well.

Boyajian has a great assortment of oils used to flavor baked goods. High-quality products and great service. Available at www.boyajianinc.com.

For all things baking, ingredients, equipment, and advice, visit www.kingarthurflour.com.

FRIENDS AND RESOURCES

www.latavolaristorante.com
www.cucinacasalinga.com
www.middleburyconsignment.com
www.scottgoodwin.com
www.intermezzomagazine.com
www.hunthillfarmtrust.org

REFERENCES

Gisslen, Wayne (2005). *Professional Baking.* Hoboken, NJ: John Wiley & Sons, Inc.
Rinsky, Glenn, and Pinsky, Laura Halpin (2009). *The Pastry Chef's Companion,* Hoboken, NJ: John Wiley & Sons, Inc.

Index